POLITICAL RISK MANAGEMENT

Recent Titles from Quorum Books

Successful Corporate Turnarounds: A Guide for Board Members, Financial Managers, Financial Institutions, and Other Creditors
Eugene F. Finkin

Drawing the Line on Natural Gas Regulation: The Harvard Study on the Future of Natural Gas
Joseph P. Kalt and Frank C. Schuller, editors

Managing the Media: Proactive Strategy for Better Business-Press Relations
Fred J. Evans

Environmental Law and Policy in the People's Republic of China
Lester Ross and Mitchell A. Silk

The Corporate Speech Writer's Handbook: A Guide for Professionals in Business, Agencies, and the Public Sector
Jerry Tarver

International Countertrade
Christopher M. Korth, editor

Accounting Principles for the Autonomous Corporate Entity
Henry P. Hill

Microcomputers as Decision Aids in Law Practice
Stuart S. Nagel

Communicating Employee Responsibilities and Rights: A Modern Management Mandate
Chimezie A. B. Osigweh, Yg., editor

The Future of Hong Kong: Toward 1997 and Beyond
Hungdah Chiu, Y. C. Jao, and Yuan-li Wu, editors

Corporate Financial Planning and Management in a Deficit Economy
Louis E. V. Nevaer and Steven A. Deck

Encouraging Cooperation among Competitors: The Case of Motor Carrier Deregulation and Collective Ratemaking
William B. Tye

CHARLES R. KENNEDY, JR.

POLITICAL RISK MANAGEMENT

INTERNATIONAL LENDING AND INVESTING UNDER ENVIRONMENTAL UNCERTAINTY

Q

QUORUM BOOKS

NEW YORK • WESTPORT, CONNECTICUT • LONDON

Library of Congress Cataloging-in-Publication Data

Kennedy, Charles R.
Political risk management.

Includes index.
1. Investments, American. 2. Corporations, American. 3. Loans, American. 4. Risk management—United States. 5. Country risk. I. Title.
HG4538.K44 1987 332.6′7373 86-25588
ISBN 0-89930-157-6 (lib. bdg. : alk. paper)

Library of Congress Catalog Card Number: 86-25588
ISBN: 0-89930-157-6

First published in 1987 by Quorum Books

Greenwood Press, Inc.
88 Post Road West, Westport, Connecticut 06881

Printed in the United States of America

The paper used in this book complies with the Permanent Paper Standard issued by the National Information Standards Organization (Z39.48-1984).

10 9 8 7 6 5 4 3 2 1

Copyright Acknowledgment

The author gratefully acknowledges permission to reprint the following:

Figure 3 is from Douglas Hibbs, *Mass Political Violence: A Cross-National Causal Analysis*, copyright © 1973 by John Wiley & Sons, Inc. Reprinted by permission of John Wiley & Sons, Inc.

Figure 4 is from Thomas N. Gladwin and Ingo Walter, *Multinationals Under Fire*, copyright © 1980 by John Wiley & Sons, Inc. Reprinted by permission of John Wiley & Sons, Inc.

This book is dedicated to J.D.H.,
a great friend and novelist

Contents

Figures and Tables

Figures

Tables

Abbreviations

ASEAN	Association of Southeast Asian Nations
BAM	Brazil, Argentina, Mexico
BERI	Business Environmental Risk Index
BI	Business International
BIS	Bank for International Settlements
CPI	Consumer Price Index
EEC	European Economic Community
ESP	Economic, Social, and Political Risk Assessment Program
FDI	Foreign Direct Investment
GATT	General Agreement on Tariffs and Trade
GDP	Gross Domestic Product
GNP	Gross National Product
GSP	General System of Tariff Preferences
IMF	International Monetary Fund (also, the Fund)
IMS	Issues Monitoring System
LDC	Less Developed Country
LIBOR	London Interbank Offer Rate
NBI	Nikkei's Business Index
NIEO	New International Economic Order
OECD	Organization of Economic Cooperation and Development
OMA	Orderly Marketing Agreement
OPEC	Organization of Petroleum Exporting Countries

PRISM	Primary Risk Investment Screening Matrix
PRI	Political Risk Index
PSSI	Political System Stability Index
ROI	Return on Investment
SAL	Structural Adjustment Loan
SBU	Strategic Business Unit
WPRF	World Political Risk Forecasts

POLITICAL RISK MANAGEMENT

1

History and Concepts

Managing political risk has become an increasingly important function within major U.S. firms over the last decade and a half. In large part this trend followed the growing turbulence and uncertainty in the firms' external international environment, a turbulence whose beginning was symbolized by the 1973–74 oil shock. This heightened importance of political risk analysis is true for U.S. banks and multinational, industrial corporations. Both types of firms have been negatively affected by the rising tide of international turmoil and volatility.

As the importance of and corporate resources devoted to formal political risk analysis increased, the level of managerial confidence in various known approaches to political risk management tended to decline. Making such analysis relevant to corporate decision making was also a problem. A large gap developed between the need for good political risk management and the ability to deliver it. This book is designed to help close or narrow that gap by providing a report on the political risk management practices of U.S. multinationals—both banking and industrial—and by using this information to develop a suggested approach to political risk management. Thus the book attempts not only to describe how U.S. firms manage political risk, but to prescribe how companies should be doing it as well.

To this end, the current chapter identifies historical political risk trends and defines key concepts. Without clear, precise definitions and explicitly drawn relationships to guide analysis, problems of wrong data selection, inappropriate use of analytical tools, and misinterpretation of findings can result. The second chapter investigates current political risk practices within U.S. banks, and the strengths and weaknesses of past and present approaches. On the basis of that analysis the third chapter presents a conceptual scheme for the classification of country risk analysis and a decision-making matrix for international lending. Similarly, the fourth chapter describes current political risk management activities of U.S. multinational, industrial corporations in order to develop a strategic management approach for industrial firms, presented in the fifth chapter. The final chapter deals with future directions in political risk management and includes discussions of scenario development for the international debt crisis and the role of multinational corporations in the evolving world political economy.

U.S. MULTINATIONAL CORPORATIONS: POLITICAL RISK TRENDS

One of the first comprehensive studies investigating the extent to which U.S. multinational corporations formally analyze political risk was conducted by Franklin Root in the late 1960s. He found that virtually no large U.S. firm had assigned any formal responsibility for the function even though nearly all firms stated that the external environment was one of the most important determinants of business success or failure.[1] Yair Aharoni reported similar findings at about the same time.[2] By 1978, a study sponsored by the Conference Board and headed by Stephen Kobrin revealed a dramatic change in this respect: 55 percent of a 193-firm sample had formally institutionalized political risk analysis in one or more departments or individuals.[3] By 1983, a new study seemed to confirm continuation of this trend toward more formalized political risk studies in large U.S. corporations, with 74 percent of a 61-firm sample having institutionalized or focused responsibility for this function somewhere in the firm.[4]

The underlying causes of this rise in formal political risk analysis are manifold. Most basic is the rapid internationalization of U.S. firms in the post–World War II period. As American business was conducted in more and more countries, political risk conditions became more complex, more important, and less familiar. At the same time that U.S. firms were moving rapidly abroad, there was a concomitant increase in nationalism among host countries, both in extent and in intensity. Not only did the number of independent countries grow with the decolonization process, but nationalistic sentiments exploded as well. This more pervasive and intense nationalism was in part a reaction to the legacy of colonialism, but a more fundamental, long-term cause was the growing interdependence of the world political economy. As each nation became more affected by and aware of political and economic developments abroad, defensive nationalistic reactions became more common. Interdependence also added more complexity and uncertainty to the corporate external environment. The 1973–74 Organization of Petroleum Exporting Countries (OPEC) embargo and price hike was the symbolic confluence of the two interrelated trends. In fact many multinational corporations cite that event as what triggered the upsurge in formal political risk analysis.

Rising nationalism was expressed in ways other than macroeconomic shocks. Forced divestments or expropriations of corporate assets began to rise in the same period. The number of forced divestments had averaged around three per year since the late 1940s to 1969, but during the early and mid–1970s, the average jumped more than fourfold. The external corporate environment was becoming not only more complex and uncertain, it was becoming directly hostile as well. Multinational corporations, as the most active and visible expressions of interdependence, became the lightning rods for nationalistic reaction.

The U.S. government, moreover, was increasingly unable to intervene or guarantee the safety of American investments abroad. Since the early 1970s, U.S. military preponderance was no longer a geopolitical fact. Certainly, many host governments took this into consideration when expropriating U.S. corporate property, as did OPEC when initiating the oil embargo.

Rising nationalism was also manifested by greater political instability in foreign countries, epitomized by the Iranian revolution of 1978–79. Contrary to some perceptions in the media, however, the impact of Iran on political risk management by U.S. corporations was more qualitative than quantitative. There has not been a great upsurge in the number of U.S. firms doing formal political risk analysis since Iran.[5] The progression of systematic political risk management has been more or less linear, starting in the early and mid–1970s and continuing into the 1980s. The major change since the fall of the Shah has instead been in the way political risk analysis is undertaken. During the 1980s, such analysis is increasingly focused in one department, usually strategic planning, and is the responsibility of full-time analysts. This contrasts with the tendency in the 1970s to disperse responsibility in more than one department and to give individuals only part-time responsibilities toward assessing political risk.

Qualitative changes within U.S. corporations, along with the increase in internationalization, also stimulated formal political risk analysis. Given the technological transformation in communication and transportation systems, today's multinational corporations find it more feasible to plan and implement global strategies, and external environmental factors have always been considered key ingredients of any corporate strategy. As global planning activities increased, so did formal political risk analysis, which in many corporations started at about the same time they began to adopt portfolio planning systems. In particular as strategic business unit (SBU) concepts were utilized, the institutionalization of political risk analysis tends to follow.

U.S. INTERNATIONAL BANKS: COUNTRY RISK TRENDS

U.S. international banks have followed a pattern of experience and adaptation vis-à-vis the international political environment similar to that of U.S. multinational corporations. Instead of political risk, however, banks prefer to discuss external environmental issues in terms of country risk. *Political risk*, a subset of country risk, can be defined as a political event that causes financial, strategic or personnel losses for a firm, whereas *country risk* refers to elements of risk inherent in doing business in the economic, social and political environment of another country. Since social, political, and economic phenomena are highly interrelated and often inseparable, this book will sometimes use these terms interchangeably.[6]

Like U.S. multinational corporations, banks started to formalize country risk analysis after the first oil shock. A fairly stable and certain environment began changing much more rapidly and unpredictably. As William Butcher, chief executive officer for Chase Manhattan, said, "The world prior to 1973 was somewhat simpler economically and politically. Since that time, the risks have escalated."[7] Another banker observed, "we always did country evaluations on a more or less informal basis, but after the first oil shock, it became clear we had to evaluate things more carefully."[8]

The first major U.S. bank to institutionalize the country risk function was Citibank in 1974. By 1976 an Export-Import Bank study by Jerome Blask indicated that of thirty-seven major U.S. banks sampled, including the twelve largest, thirty-two had a systematic approach to country risk analysis.[9] Thus the spread of formal country risk management within U.S. banks was quite rapid after 1973.

The impact of Iran on U.S. banks was significant as well. As with U.S. multinational corporations, the reaction of banks, in their country risk management practices, was more qualitative than quantitative. That is, the Iranian revolution was not followed by a noticeable increase in the number of banks doing formal country risk analysis, but many banks already doing such analysis changed their approach. In particular sociopolitical factors were upgraded in importance relative to macroeconomic considerations. As Joseph Tunney, the vice president in charge of country risk at Chemical Bank, said, "Iran was a watershed, making us appreciate that our . . . approach to political analysis had to change."[10]

Banks, however, were uncertain how to integrate political variables into macroeconomic analysis. Such integration was particularly difficult for bankers since the vast majority before 1978 were using a structured qualitative model, in the attempt to draw explicit relationships between qualitative, sociopolitical data and quantitative, economic data. When political factors were assumed insignificant, the difficulties in using structured qualitative approaches were not great. In other words, political variables before Iran tended to be considered only peripherally to macroeconomic analysis. After the Iranian revolution, however, political factors had to be more centrally and systematically integrated into macroeconomics. As a result, a large shift occurred in the predominant methodology used by banks toward country analysis. By the early 1980s, most major U.S. banks had adopted checklist systems, in which economic and political variables are listed, weighted, and then ranked during each round of analysis. A composite score is generated and used to classify countries as to their riskiness. Bankers were naturally attracted to checklist systems because they easily facilitated systematic integration of political and economic factors.

With the explosion of the international debt crisis in 1982, the perceived need among bankers for better country risk analysis grew even greater. A recent study of twenty-nine major banks revealed that most had employed "more resources

. . . to conduct in-depth country risk analysis'' since 1982.[11] At the same time, several concerned bankers were somewhat disillusioned with checklist systems because of their failure to help predict the major crises of 1982, particularly Mexico and Argentina. Many bankers also became more skeptical about their ability to correctly forecast sociopolitical events. As a result, there has been some visible movement recently among banks toward short-term, econometric models. International lending decisions, however, must often consider the risks over a longer period of time than econometric models are designed to predict; econometric models are also limited by not including important socioeconomic variables. Bankers understand this, for no major U.S. bank solely relies on econometric models when doing country risk analysis. In short banks are generally dissatisfied with existing approaches to country risk.

TYPES OF POLITICAL RISK EVENTS

A political risk event is one that threatens a firm with a financial, strategic or personnel loss due to non-market forces. A political event in itself does not necessarily constitute a risk to business. Even revolution as the most dramatic form of ''political instability is neither a necessary nor a sufficient condition for changes in policy relevant to foreign investment.''[12] In fact political instability can present opportunities as well as risks to business. For example, Gulf Oil Corporation in 1975 was able to negotiate a very favorable relationship with the Marxist MPLA during the Angolan civil war, and Dow Chemical was able to reenter Chile after the overthrow of Salvador Allende in 1973.

Definitions of political risk, therefore, that focus on environmental uncertainties or changes as such are misplaced.[13] Such definitions can encourage managers to focus their attention on trying to predict the likelihood of certain significant political changes, which might or might not have an impact on the firm. This broad traditional approach to political risk assessment by U.S. firms ''can be generally characterized as unsophisticated, subjective and made in general rather than investment specific terms.''[14] Managers and consultants have tended to stress prediction of a limited number of political events—war, revolutionary expropriations, and exchange controls. In recent years, however,

> political risk studies have been expanding to include numerous other specific types of risks whose origins lie at least partly in political processes. . . . This expansion will probably continue since virtually all risks faced by firms are directly or indirectly related to political processes. Indeed, nearly all of a firm's interests are affected by politics.[15]

The global marketplace is by its very nature uncertain and turbulent. Whether or not particular aspects of this turbulence and uncertainty constitute a risk to business is problematic and depends on industry, firm or project characteristics and managerial actions. Gulf in Angola clearly faced an uncertain, turbulent investment environment but was able to avoid political risk or politically related losses because of certain managerial, proactive decisions. Reflecting such experiences, "the trend in definitions and empirical analyses in political risk studies has been toward an emphasis on the actual impact of firms' interests."[16]

The linkage between political events and risks, therefore, is often rooted in managerial decisions or the absence thereof. Political turbulence and uncertainty can be proactively managed into targets of competitive opportunity, but in order for this to occur, the firm must understand the multidimensional and complex nature of political risk. Political risk can have an economic, sociocultural or purely political source. In our definition of political risk, these are all non-market forces. For example, a country's policy decision to tighten or expand foreign investment laws or to renege on international debt obligations is often preceded and precipitated by an economic, balance-of-payments disequilibrium. Of course, these balance-of-payment difficulties may be partially rooted in sociopolitical factors, such as widespread corruption and public sector mismanagement. The case of Zaire aptly demonstrates these particular economic-sociopolitical relationships.[17] As Root correctly observed, the distinction between purely economic and political risks has only analytical usefulness and breaks down at the operational level.[18] Sociocultural, political, and economic phenomena are highly and dynamically interrelated.[19]

Political risk analysts, therefore, cannot simply concentrate on purely political factors and events, the traditional focus of formal assessments by corporations. Managers must systematically analyze the varied and possible sources of political risk. Such analysis can be aided greatly by a conceptual framework that explicitly interrelates sociocultural, political, and economic factors.

A later chapter will present such a framework, but a manager should also be aware of the range or types of political risk events that can emanate from these many sources. They begin with the obvious trauma of revolutionary upheaval. For example, in December 1977, GTE signed a telecommunications contract worth more than $500 million with the Iranian government. In accordance with the contract, GTE advanced Iran $94 million in open letters of credit, commonly used in the Middle East in lieu of performance bonds. Given its long-time experience and confidence in Iran, the company did virtually nothing to protect itself from possible political risks and, therefore, the contract did not specify the grounds on which Iran could call the letters of credit, and no insurance was taken to cover their risks. After the revolution, work on their project proved impossible, and the company stood to lose over $50 million, not including those worrisome letters of credit. If those are included, GTE's potential after-tax losses exceed $60 million, making the firm the biggest potential loser in Iran.

Many types of political risk events exist besides those caused by revolutions or coups. Some companies, for example, were victims of political risk in Iran before the revolution. Acts of terrorism while the Shah was still in power were one form of such risk, with the murder of Rockwell International employees being the most dramatic example. Besides acts of violence against the state or

Figure 1
Types of Political Risks

MACRO	Revolution	Investment Laws
MICRO	Terrorism	Trade Regulations
	Extra-Legal	Legal-Governmental

individual companies, political risk can also take the form of legislative or regulatory changes. In Iran B.F. Goodrich had built the largest tire plant between Europe and the Far East, with assurances of trade and investment protection from the government, but such protection was prematurely lifted in favor of two competitors in the mid–1970s, forcing the U.S. firm to go from a three-shift to a single eight-hour production schedule. Changes in the law or in regulations can also be directed at all or most companies collectively, as when the Shah in the 1970s decided to mandate public stock offerings on the part of Iranian-based corporations so as to increase worker ownership and participation. The action was expensive and very disruptive to foreign businesses.

The many different kinds of political risk events that exist can be broadly divided into either extra-legal or legal-governmental risk, and either macro or micro risk. Extra-legal risk includes any event that is sourced from outside the existing authority or legitimacy structure of the state, such as terrorism, sabotage, military coups, or revolutions. Legal-governmental risk, however, is a direct product of the ongoing political process and includes such events as democratic elections leading to a new government or changes in the law concerning trade, labor, joint-venture, subsidy, technology, monetary, and developmental policies. Macro risk events affect all or nearly all firms adversely, while micro risk affects only a select few or individual firms.

These classifications can yield a matrix of possible political risk events, as shown in Figure 1 for the Iranian situation. The overthrow of the Shah was a macro, extra-legal political risk event; it affected nearly all foreign firms adversely and similarly. The revolution, in fact, resulted in potential losses for American-based firms exceeding $1 billion. Terrorism is also an extra-legal risk incident but one that typically affects only a few unfortunate firms. The underlying causes of terrorism and revolution, however, are very similar. The Shah's 1975 decree that 49 percent of share ownership should be held by the public so that employees could better participate in their firm's management decisions and profits is instead an example of macro, legal-governmental risk. Nearly all foreign firms in Iran were potentially and adversely affected by the decree since stock offerings to workers were at concessionary rates and the multinationals lost much of their managerial control in the process. Political risk that is sourced from the ongoing political process can also be directed at individual companies, as in the B.F. Goodrich example. A complete political risk assessment needs to address all these possibilities.

Extra-legal risk assignment, however, is the most basic place for an analyst to start. If such risk is of the macro variety, such as from a revolution, then there is a good chance that the political system's laws and regulations toward foreign business will be altered as well. If there is a high probability of macro, extra-legal risk or if the political elite is facing serious challenges to its rule, then the host government is more likely to change laws and regulations affecting multinational corporations as an attempt to win public support. Thus the presence of extra-legal risk can lead to legal-governmental changes that may threaten the firm.

POLITICAL RISK APPROACHES AND THE IRANIAN REVOLUTION

The Iranian revolution was the most traumatic foreign political event ever faced by U.S. firms. It was particularly traumatic not only because of the huge losses but because the losses were completely unexpected by most firms. For this reason, and with a view toward facilitating construction of an improved model of political risk, it may be highly instructive to examine past political risk approaches in terms of their strengths and weaknesses in predicting the revolution.

The Ex-Im Bank study of U.S. banks in 1976 found four general approaches to country risk assessment: qualitative and unstructured (where no standard format or system exists), structured qualitative, checklist, and econometric. Another related way to summarize different approaches to political risk analysis is to construct a matrix relating qualitative-quantitative approaches to those that are either theoretical or nontheoretical, as shown in Figure 2.

Unstructured qualitative approaches are obviously nontheoretical and dependent on subjective judgment and expert opinion. The best structured qualitative models are based on an interrelated set of variables (a conceptual model) supported by empirical evidence as being significantly related to political risk. In this sense structured qualitative models have a theoretical base as do econometric models. Checklist systems, on the other hand, have little or no theoretical justification for their weighting and ranking procedures. Attaching 20 to 40 percent of the total weight to political versus economic factors, for example, has no theoretical basis.

Other classification schemes are also represented within Figure 2. R. J. Rum-

Figure 2
Political Risk Approaches

	Qualitative	Quantitative
Theoretical	Structured qualitative Components	Econometric quantitative methods Empirical-formal observational
Non-Theoretical	Unstructured qualitative Checklist Grand tours Old hands Delphi/expert-generated opinion	"Coin-flips"

mel and David Heenan classified political risk approaches into four categories: ''grand tours,'' in which top management visits foreign countries; ''old hands,'' for which the opinions of those with experience or expertise in the country are collected; ''Delphi'' approaches, when expert opinions are solicited through a structured interviewing format; and quantitative methods.[20]

Another classification scheme divides political risk approaches into three groups: expert-generated opinion, component, and empirical-formal observational.[21] Expert-generated opinion approaches can be of the grand tour, old hands, or Delphi type—all, of course, are qualitative and nontheoretical.

A component approach, however, is a structured qualitative model that attempts to measure and relate the essential ingredients of political risk. This approach chooses structural causes of political risk and then attempts to measure the variables objectively, although a degree of objective-subjective interaction is always required. Besides being more objective and theoretically based than expert-generated opinion approaches, a component model presents the additional advantage that sources of political risk and their potential impact on the firm are more clearly identified and can be better assessed.

Like component approaches, formal-empirical observational models attempt to measure the structural causes of political risk, but unlike either expert-generated opinion or component approaches, they avoid subjective analysis. Only hard, observational data that have been empirically and statistically tested are used. Quantitative scores are generated and are compared across countries.

Three examples of expert-generated opinion approaches are the Business Environmental Risk Index (BERI), the Business International (BI) system, and Nikkei's Business Index (NBI). BERI (currently called the Operations Risk Index) uses fifteen variables that are thought to be related to political risk. These variables and their respective weights are shown in Table 1.

As Table 1 shows, the sum total of the weights is 25 and each variable is scored at four times its weight so that 100 is the total possible points for a

Table 1
BERI Variables and Weights

Variables	Weights
Political Stability	3
Foreign Investment Attitude	1 1/2
Nationalization	1 1/2
Monetary Inflation	1 1/2
Balance of Payments	1 1/2
Bureaucratic Delays	1
Economic Growth	2 1/2
Currency Convertibility	2 1/2
Contract Enforceability	1 1/2
Labor Cost/Productivity	2
Professional Support	1/2
Communications/Transportation	1
Local Management	1
Short-Term Credit	2
Long-Term Capital	2

Source: F.T. Haner, "Business Environment Risk Index, Appendix B," BERI Ltd. System for Selected Countries, August 1981, p. 9.

country. One hundred also represents the lowest possible risk. BERI is thus a checklist type of system which structures expert-generated opinion.

To obtain these ratings, the Delphi interviewing method is used with a permanent panel of experts, who number over one hundred and reside in the United States and in each target country. Each panelist subjectively assesses a quantified score for each variable for a particular country, and after initial answers, is informed of the mean response of other panelists. Adjustments in scores can then be made. A final score for a country is obtained by throwing out the highest and lowest scores and then averaging the rest. Around forty-five countries are covered each year, with the range of country scores falling between the low 30s to low 80s. A mean in the 60s has been the norm; scores between 70 and 56 have been called moderate risks, which meant that complications would arise in day-to-day operations but "the structure of the political environment is sufficiently stable to permit change without seriously damaging the business environment."[22]

BI used a similar Delphi procedure; however, the manner in which experts scored variables differed. For example, while BERI rated a country's stability along a 0–4 continuum of unacceptable to superior, BI's experts rated political instability by choosing one of the following: a score of 15 for "guaranteed" long-term stability, 10 for a strong government with a vulnerable constitution, 5 for active internal factions, or 2 for strong probability of overthrow, either internal or external.[23] Remarkably, not only did BI and BERI use very similar methodologies, but their predictions were highly correlated as well. In the 1972–

Table 2
PSSI Indices and Operational Variables

I. Socioeconomic Index

   A. Ethnolinguistic fractionalism
   B. GNP growth per capita
   C. Energy consumption per capita

II. Societal Conflict Index

   A. Public Unrest Subindex
      1. riots
      2. demonstrations
      3. government crises

   B. Internal Violence Subindex
      1. armed attacks
      2. assassinations
      3. coups d'etat
      4. guerrilla warfare

   C. Coercion Potential Subindex
      1. internal security forces per 1000

III. Governmental Processes Index

   A. Political competition index
   B. Legislative effectiveness
   C. Constitutional changes per year
   D. Irregular chief executive changes

Source: Dan Haendel, Foreign Investments and the Management of Political Risk (Boulder: Westview Press, 1979), p. 108.

74 period, for example, the forecasts of the two models had a coefficient of 0.894.[24]

A third expert-generated opinion approach that existed before the Iranian revolution was NBI, which can be seen as the Japanese version of BI and BERI. NBI ranked the investment appeal of fifty-three countries for Japanese firms in 1977. Even though two different assessments were made, one for market-oriented enterprises and the other for resource-processing companies, the same type of political risk rating was subjectively made in either case. The lowest risk score was 100, whereas moderately and highly risky countries were given scores of 66 and 33, respectively.

Two component models were known publicly before the Iranian revolution. One, developed by Dan Haendel and Gerald West, was called the Political System Stability Index (PSSI).[25] Three equally weighted indices were used to generate an overall score, either a positive or negative number. The more negative the number, the greater the political risk. These indices were determined by ratings of numerous variables, as Table 2 shows.

All of PSSI's operational variables are measured quantitatively, which leads to an aggregate number or score for the country, yet these quantitative methods are guided by a number of subjective considerations. Most basic is that the variables and their interrelationships are not fully supported by empirical theory, particularly the decision to give equal weighting to the three main indices. This decision perhaps gave undue weight to the governmental processes index, which has a definite liberal-democratic bias.

A second component model also suffered from the same kind of bias. Even though Robert Green astutely focused on the interrelationship between political structures and political stability in modernizing societies, his assumptions regarding the relative stability of various political systems are questionable. According to Green, modernizing liberal democratic regimes are the most stable, followed by modernizing autocracies, military dictatorships, mass mobilization regimes, and newly independent states.[26] This ranking of relative stability was not empirically tested, but rather subjectively assumed.

Two major empirical-formal observational models existed before the Iranian revolution. One such model was developed by Harald Knudsen and is derived from the ''J-Curve'' theory of revolutions developed primarily by James Davies and Ted Gurr. Knudsen called his model the ''ecological approach,'' and based it on the proposition that the crucial measure of stability was the frustration level in a society.[27] By comparing the level of aspiration to welfare/expectation levels, one derived a frustration gap between the two. In particular when welfare/expectation levels drop quickly and dramatically as aspiration levels hold steady or grow, a large frustration gap or J-Curve develops, significantly raising the probability of revolution. The operational variables for this model are listed in Table 3.

The other empirical-formal observational model was initially developed by Douglas Hibbs in 1973 and then applied to political risk analysis by Rummel and Heenan in 1978. Hibbs developed a causal model of mass political violence by employing factor and regression analysis.[28] Only variables that were strongly supported by major qualitative theories about political change were statistically tested using data from 108 countries. If variables were found to have coefficients of at least twice their respective standard errors, they were incorporated into the causal model, illustrated by Figure 3.

Hibbs generated a causal model of instability that had a multiblock recursive structure. As one can see, many variables were used to determine the relative probability of collective protest (operationalized as the number of riots, general strikes, and antigovernment demonstrations) and/or internal war (operationalized as the number of armed attack events, assassinations, and deaths from political violence). This model stood alone in categorizing Iran as having a high potential for political instability, as shown in Table 4. In terms of both collective protest and internal war, Iran was rated as one of the most politically unstable countries in the world, as indicated by statistical Z scores. These scores indicated that

Table 3
Ecological Approach Variables

I. Aspiration Level

A. Literacy rate
B. Daily newspaper circulation per 1,000 population
C. Radios per 1,000 population
D. Relative urbanization
E. Labor unionization

II. Welfare-Expectation Level

A. Infant mortality rate
B. Hospital beds per 1,000 population
C. Doctors per 10,000 population
D. Piped water supply per capita
E. GNP per capita
F. Percent change in per capita GNP
G. Gross investment rates as a percent of GNP

Source: Harold Knudson, "Explaining the National Propensity to Expropriate: An Ecological Approach," Journal of International Business Studies, Spring 1974, pp. 53-55.

Iran's potentials for collective protest and internal war were within the top 17 and 15 percent of all countries, respectively.

BI's political stability rating for Iran, on the other hand, gave no warning of problems. For instance, the rating for Iran's political risk remained low, at 10 from 1971–77, that is, the Iranian government was considered strong but had a vulnerable constitution. The rating in 1978 fell to a 5, indicating the presence of active internal factions, and then to a 2 the next year, after the revolution in essence had occurred.[29] A flaw of the BI system, like so many other models, is centered in its strong liberal democratic bias, generated in part by many of the experts who make the predictions, but also embodied in the model itself. The question needed to be asked whether a category containing the criterion of a "strong government with a vulnerable constitution" made sense in the context of the Shah's Iran.

BERI similarly gave Iran only a moderately risky rating, a 58 in 1975, a 60 in 1976, and a 58 in both 1977 and 1978. Although these scores were at the more risky end of the moderate risk category (70–56), this was due to legal-governmental risk concerns, not extra-legal or political instability factors. As BERI's *Executive Guide to Conducting Business in Iran* stated: "The primary problem is the fluid nature of contracts, regulations, government decisions, and so on."[30] The political stability variable instead was given a low risk rating of 2.9 out of 3 points. As the BERI report on Iran said, the Shah "represents long-

Figure 3
Hibbs' Causal Model with Path Coefficient

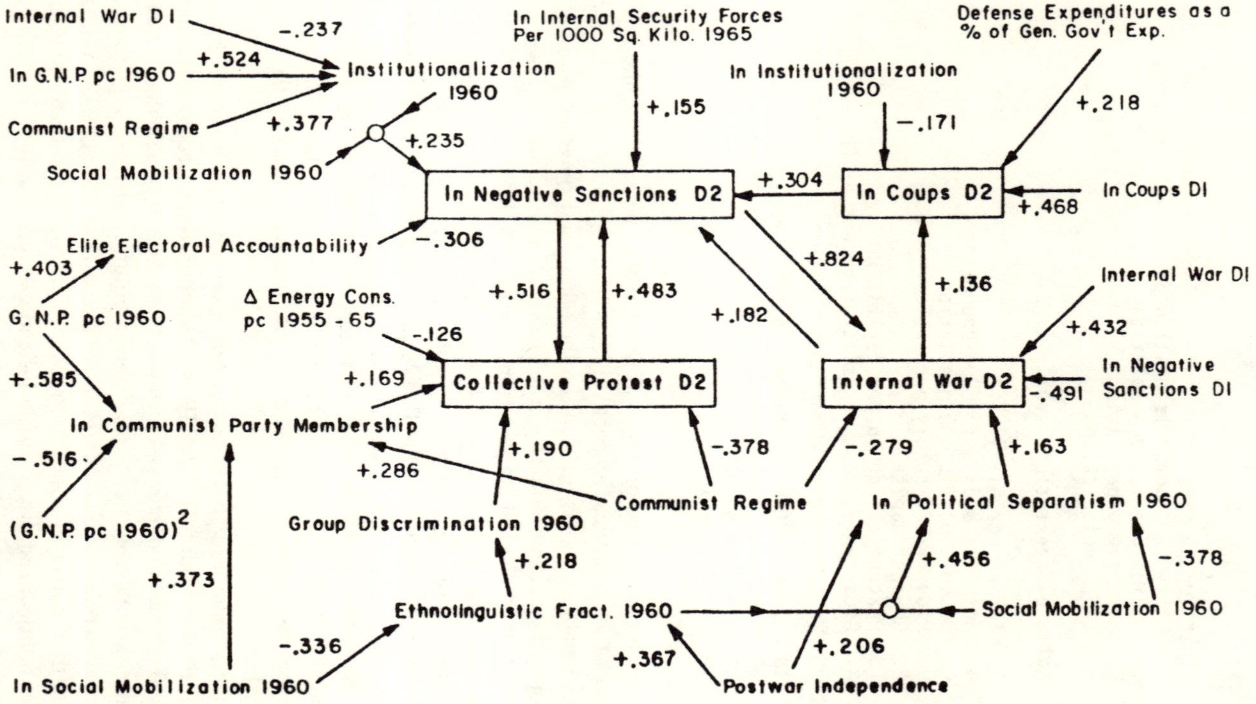

Source: Douglas Hibbs, Mass Political Violence: A Cross-National Causal Analysis (New York: John Wiley and Sons, 1973), p. 181.

Table 4
Hibbs' Instability Ratings

Country	Collective Protest	Internal War
Iran	4.548	7.421
Iraq	3.894	7.075
Saudi Arabia	2.082	0.983
108-country mean	3.234	4.734
Standard deviation	1.389	2.671
Iran z score	.949	1.010

Adapted from Douglas Hibbs, Mass Political Violence: A Cross-National Causal Analysis (New York: John Wiley and Sons, 1973), pp. 239-44.

range progress and increasing power for Iran. . . . As a result, the Shah and his policies have broad-based support within the country.''[31]

NBI also failed to warn corporations that Iran was a high political risk. Iran received a moderate political risk rating of 66 for both of NBI's industry categories. All other Middle East countries rated by NBI—Iraq, Saudi Arabia, Kuwait, Algeria, and Egypt—received the same score.[32]

The two component models fared no better than expert-generated opinion approaches. The Green analysis of political structures proved misleading, as it rated Iran to be one of the most stable countries in the Middle East. Given that all the lower Gulf sheikdoms were newly independent and Iraq and Syria were mass mobilizational regimes, they should have been more unstable than Iran. In addition two of the more liberal democratic governments in the area, Pakistan and Lebanon, both experienced violent internal upheavals in the 1970s, which again contradicted Green's analysis.

The other component model, PSSI, did not fare much better. The only published score for Iran was −0.61 and was based on 1961–66 data.[33] There were sixty other countries rated, with a mean score of 0.21 and a standard deviation of 0.95. Iran was within a half a standard deviation from the mean, hardly an extraordinarily high political risk relative to other countries.

One could also argue that if the PSSI model had rated Iran based on 1971–76 data, then the country would certainly have received an even more positive rating. The socioeconomic index, which had a −0.34 score, would have become more positive because of the growth in GNP and energy consumption during the 1970s. The societal conflict index, which had a −0.31 score, would also have become more positive in the 1970s since the number of riots and demonstrations during the White Revolution period of the 1960s far exceeded those in the years before the revolution. The governmental processes index would have become more positive as well, given the continued longevity of the Shah.

The Knudsen ''ecological approach'' proved misleading as well. Knudsen's approach failed to predict a high probability of revolution in Iran primarily because welfare/expectation variables did not decline in relation to aspiration. In fact the most important welfare/expectation variables, GNP per capita and its rate of change, continued to climb until the eve of the 1978–79 revolution. In effect there was no visible, downward "J" in the revolutionary curve.

Several factors could explain why the Hibbs model stood alone in forecasting a high probability of revolution in Iran. The most important explanation related to the model's comprehensive testing of most qualitative theories of instability. Knudsen's empirical tests were simply very limited in scope and predetermined by a prior, largely deductive, theory. Hibbs' model, on the other hand, assumed no validity for any previous theory and was erected empirically from the ground up. As a result, theoretical preconceptions or value biases were avoided; for instance, liberal-democratic bias was completely discarded in the recognition that totalitarian communist regimes significantly reduce the occurrence of both collective protest and internal war (path coefficients of −.378 and −.279, respectively).

Besides the comprehensive testing of many hypotheses and theories about political instability, the Hibbs model has the additional attraction of containing most variables currently considered to be key ingredients for understanding revolutionary change. These include the type of political system; the degree of ethnolinguistic factionalism, group discrimination, or congruent cleavages; the degree of state coercive potential (PSSI's internal security force ratios) and action (negative sanctions); the presence of political separatist or revolutionary groups; the interaction between social mobilization (participation) and institutionalization (Samuel Huntington's political development model);[34] and the historic importance of major upheaval or internal war in the recent past. Not only were these variables utilized, but their interactive relationship was tested empirically. Any future model of political risk would need to incorporate many of these same variables and interrelationships.

It is interesting to note that the F. T. Haner organization started doing just that immediately before the revolution in Iran occurred. In 1976, a new political risk approach, the Political Risk Index (PRI), was tested vis-à-vis Iran. (PRI contained ten variables, most of them found in the Hibbs model.) Since Iran was rated a 46 out of a possible 100 points in the first trial test, the country fell within the high risk category (40–54 points). Haner found the discrepancy between the BERI and PRI scores disturbing, and as a result, 18 further months of PRI trials followed. After changing the composition of the panel of experts, the 1977 and 1978 PRI scores showed a worsening political risk situation, with Iran rated a 43 in 1977 and a 37 in 1978. In fact the first publicized rating for Iran was a 34 in the fall of 1978. Both ratings in 1978 were classified as "prohibitive risks."[35] It is perhaps not a coincidence that the two political risk approaches that used many of the same variables were the only ones that made similarly negative forecasts about Iran's stability under the Shah.

POLITICAL RISK APPROACHES AND NEEDS IN THE 1980S

Despite the trauma of Iran, a major and rising concern of corporate political risk managers is legal-governmental, not extra-legal risk. There have undoubtedly been greater corporate financial losses caused by legal-governmental risk events than by revolutions, coups, or terrorism since World War II. This is particularly true for banks since mid–1982, when the events in Mexico led to the explosion of the international debt crisis.

Given the importance of legal-governmental risk, political risk approaches developed in the 1980s had to deal increasingly with economic policy forecasts and bargaining-power analysis. Two approaches should be mentioned. World Political Risk Forecasts (WPRF), developed by Michael O'Leary and William Coplin,[36] is based on the theory of group politics.[37] WPRF rates countries by expert-generated opinion on that theoretical basis. One can attempt to forecast any economic policy issue with their system, which O'Leary and Coplin call the "Prince Model." The first step in applying the model to a country and policy issue is to survey experts concerning who are the major actors on an issue according to four criteria: orientation or position on the issue; the certainty, coherence, or firmness of the actor's orientation; the actor's power to influence the outcome on the issue; and the salience or importance of the issue to the actor. Each actor's orientation on an issue is either positive, negative, or neutral. If positive or negative, a plus or minus sign is given to the actor's overall score, which is calculated by a multiplication of the scores for the other criteria. Certainty, power, and salience variables each receive a score of one to five—the higher the number the more powerful and certain the actor is toward the issue or the more salient the issue is to the actor. A total of ±125 points for each actor is possible. Total points for all actors, ignoring sign, can then be computed, and a ratio of total positive points to total points ignoring sign can produce an estimate of how probable action is on the issue or policy. Table 5 gives an example of how the model might be applied to an economic policy issue.

The WPRF system has a number of attractions, which explains why it is one of the political risk services most subscribed to by U.S. corporations today, along with the BERI and BI services. Obviously, WPRF is conducive to legal-governmental risk assessment in a structured, systematic manner, but perhaps most important, that assessment is based on a theory of politics that has a strong tradition and widespread support in the academic, political science community. WPRF also produces probability estimates that some firms may find useful.

In spite of these strengths, WPRF suffers from some basic weaknesses. Perhaps unavoidably, the probability estimates are only as strong as the accuracy of the experts. The value biases and theoretical preconceptions of experts undermine to some extent the integrity of the system. Projections by WPRF should thus be compared to conclusions reached by models that are more objectively measured.

The weighting and scoring of variables is another flaw in the system. The

Table 5
Hypothetical Prince Model Application to Mexico Regarding Exchange Controls in July 1982

Actor	(+, -, N) Position	(1-5) Power		(1-5) Saliency		(1-5) Coherence	Total
President Lopez Portillo	+	5	x	5	x	4	=+100
Finance Minister Silva Herzog	N	2	x	2	x	2	+ (8)
Director of Central Bank, Miguel Mancera	-	3	x	5	x	5	= -75
PRI Cabinet	+	3	x	2	x	1	= +6
IMF	-	1	x	5	x	4	= -20
Labor/Left (Tello)	+	2	x	5	x	5	= +50
President-Elect Madrid	-	1	x	5	x	5	= -25

Probability of Exchange Controls = $\frac{156}{284}$ = 55%

granting of equal weights to power, coherence and saliency is highly questionable. A strong case can be made that power is much more important than the other two variables in determining policy outcomes. In addition, the procedure for giving scores to the power variable disregards the role of power as a relative concept between concerned interest groups and individuals; a better procedure for capturing the relativity of power might be to quantify each actor's power score in strictly comparative terms. It could be asumed that all relevant actors on the issue represent the sum total of power being brought to bear on the issue's resolution. This sum could be represented by 100 points, and each actor would be awarded something less than 100 points, with the exact amount dependent on their power relative to others. In any case and regardless of these criticisms and possible improvements, WPRF remains an attractive system with a role to play in political risk management, particularly as a supplement to other models.

Another critical need that U.S. firms have in the area of political risk is the development of decision-making guidelines in international negotiations. Increasingly the likelihood and extent of legal-governmental risk is largely a function of the firm's characteristics and political risk-negotiation skills. This of course presents an additional problem for the O'Leary-Coplin system, which fails to integrate firm-specific variables in its policy analysis.

One approach that focuses on such an integration has been presented by Thomas Gladwin and Ingo Walter.[38] It is based on a model of conflict management developed in the field of industrial and organizational psychology. The

Figure 4
Determinants of Appropriate Conflict Behavior

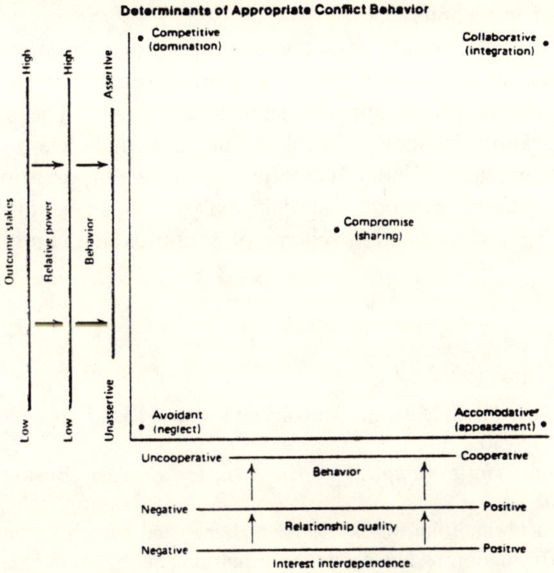

Source: Thomas N. Gladwin and Ingo Walter, Multinationals Under Fire: Lessons in the Management of Conflict (New York: John Wiley, 1980), p. 79.

Gladwin-Walter approach is illustrated in Figure 4. A matrix involving three variables on each axis was developed. On the vertical axis, one judges the outcome stakes for the firm, the firm's power relative to the adversary, and an aspect of management behavior or tactics (its assertiveness). The horizontal axis, on the other hand, contains another measure of management behavior or tactics (its cooperativeness), the quality or friendliness of the relationship, and an assessment of how interdependent the interests of the firm and the other party are. Depending upon where one ends up in the matrix, certain conflict management modes are suggested.

The Gladwin-Walter model is certainly a step in the right direction since the application of theories developed in industrial and organizational psychology to political risk management was sorely needed. The model not only facilitates the management of political risks posed by any kind of government—home, host, or supranational—but focuses managerial attention on firm-specific characteristics and behavior as well. It also assumes that the primary danger to the firm is not corporate-government conflict in itself, but the mismanagement of that conflict.

Drawbacks of the Gladwin-Walter model include, most importantly, the fact that the model is nearly impossible to operationalize because it is overly complex. Three largely unrelated variables on each axis make precise, objective measurement difficult. A more simplified, manageable model seems called for and will be discussed in Chapter 5.

A macro, conceptual model of a country's political economy is needed as well, since it is within the context of the overall macro environment that economic policy and bargaining power analysis should take place. The systematic and theoretical integration of sociopolitical factors and macroeconomic variables remains a fundamental difficulty that often prevents corporations from doing good, accurate country and political risk analysis. Such a conceptual model should also lead to a classification scheme of countries that can guide corporate decision making.

NOTES

1. Franklin Root, "U.S. Business Abroad and Political Risk," *MSU Business Topics*, Winter 1968, pp. 73–80.
2. Yair Aharoni, *The Foreign Investment Decision Process* (Boston: Harvard University Press, 1966).
3. Stephen J. Kobrin, John Basek, Stephen Blank, and Joseph La Palombara, "The Assessment and Evaluation of Noneconomic Environments by American Firms: A Preliminary Report," *Journal of International Business Studies*, Spring-Summer 1980, pp. 32–47.
4. Charles R. Kennedy, Jr., "The External Environment—Strategic Planning Interface: U.S. Multinational Corporate Practices in the 1980s," *Journal of International Business Studies*, Fall 1984, pp. 99–108.
5. "The Post-Shah Surge in Political Risk Studies," *Business Week*, December 1, 1980, p. 69; and Ronald Alsop, "More Firms Are Hiring Own Political Analysts to Limit Risks Abroad," *The Wall Street Journal*, March 30, 1981, p. 1.
6. Two scholars, in fact, tried to coin the term "country political risk" to avoid these terminological problems; see José De La Torre and David Neckar, "Forecasting Country Political Risk," *The Handbook of Forecasting: A Manager's Guide*, Spyros Makridakis and Steven Wheelwright, eds. (New York: John Wiley and Sons, 1982) pp. 326–27.
7. William Butcher, quoted in "Meet the New Breed of Banker: The Political Risk Expert," *Euromoney*, July 1980, p. 9.
8. Ibid., p. 12.
9. Jerome K. Blask, *A Survey of Country Evaluation Systems in Use*, The Export-Import Bank, December 22, 1977.
10. Joseph Tunney, quoted in Louis Kraar, "The Multinationals Get Smarter About Political Risks," *Fortune*, March 24, 1980, p. 99.
11. R. Peter DeWitt and Jeff Madura, "How Banks Assess Country Risk: A Survey," University of Central Florida, unpublished manuscript.
12. Stephen Kobrin, "Political Risk: A Review and Reconsideration," *Journal of International Business Studies*, Spring-Summer 1979, p. 74.
13. For example, see Dolph Warren Zink, *The Political Risks for Multinational Enterprise in Developing Countries* (New York: Praeger Publishers, 1973); Antoine Van

Agtmael, "Evaluating the Risks of Lending and Developing Countries," *Euromoney*, April 1976, pp. 16–30; and Stefan H. Robock, "Political Risk: Identification and Assessment," *Columbia Journal of World Business*, July–August 1971, pp. 6–20.

14. Douglas Nigh, "The Effect of Political Events on United States Direct Foreign Investment: A Pooled Time-Series Cross-Sectional Analysis," *Journal of International Business Studies*, Spring 1985, p. 4.

15. Thomas L. Brewer, "Politics, Risks and International Business," *Political Risks in International Business: New Directions for Research, Management and Public Policy*, Thomas L. Brewer, ed. (New York: Praeger Publishers, 1985), p. 7.

16. Ibid., p. 6.

17. For a case demonstration of this relationship, see *Zaire and the Debt Crisis*, UVA-G–246.

18. Franklin Root, "Analyzing Political Risks in International Business," *The Multinational Enterprise in Transition*, Ashok Kapoor and Phillip Grub, eds. (Princeton: The Darwin Press, 1972), pp. 354–65.

19. For recent discussions of political economy see Robert Gilpin, *U.S. Power and the Multinational Corporation* (New York: Basic Books, 1975), pp. 3–6; C. Fred Bergston, Robert Keohane, and Joseph Nye, "International Economics and International Politics: A Framework for Analysis," *World Politics and International Economics*, C. Fred Bergston and Lawrence Krause, eds. (Washington, D.C.: The Brookings Institute, 1975), pp. 3–35; and Joan Spero, *The Politics of International Economics Relations* (New York: St. Martin's Press, 1981), pp. 1–12.

20. R. J. Rummel and David Heenan, "How Multinationals Analyze Political Risk," *Harvard Business Review*, January-February 1978, pp. 68–71.

21. Gerald West, "A Component Approach to the Assessment of Political Risk," *The Measurement of Political Risk and Foreign Investment Strategy*, 1975, pp. 43–44.

22. F. T. Haner, "Business Environment Risk Index, Appendix B," *BERI Ltd. System for Selected Countries*, August 1981, p. 9.

23. For a discussion of Business International's approach to political risk assessment that existed before the Iranian revolution, see Charles R. Kennedy, Jr., "Multinational Corporations and Political Risk in the Persian Gulf," *International Journal of Middle East Studies*, Fall 1984, p. 393.

24. Dan Haendel, *Foreign Investments and the Management of Political Risk* (Boulder: Westview Press, 1979), p. 102.

25. Ibid., pp. 106–13.

26. Robert Green, "Political Structures as a Predictor of Radical Political Change," *Columbia Journal of World Business*, Spring 1974, pp. 31–35.

27. Harald Knudsen, "Explaining the National Propensity to Expropriate: An Ecological Approach," *Journal of International Business Studies*, Spring 1974, pp. 53–55.

28. Douglas Hibbs, *Mass Political Violence: A Cross-National Causal Analysis* (New York: John Wiley and Sons, 1973), pp. 3–17, 135–36, 181.

29. *Business International*, June 20, 1980, pp. 196–97.

30. BERI, *Executive Guide to Conducting Business in Iran*, September 1, 1975, p. 2.

31. Ibid., p. 8.

32. Nikkei Business, "Investment Appeal Rating of 53 Nations," *The Japanese Economic Journal*, August 16, 1977, pp. 116–19.

33. Haendel, *Foreign Investments*, p. 112.

34. Samuel Huntington, *Political Order in Changing Societies* (New Haven: Yale University Press, 1968), pp. 1–92.

35. Personal correspondence with F. T. Haner, November 1982.

36. William Coplin and Michael O'Leary, "The World Political Risk Forecasting Service," *Political Risks in International Business*, Thomas L. Brewer, ed. (New York: Praeger Publishers, 1985), pp. 163–92.

37. For a discussion of group politics, see James Bill and Robert Hardgrave, Jr., *Comparative Politics: The Quest for Theory* (Columbus: Charles E. Merrill Publishing Company, 1973), pp. 117–41.

38. Thomas Gladwin and Ingo Walter, *Multinationals Under Fire: Lessons in the Management of Conflict* (New York: John Wiley and Sons, 1980), pp. 66–89.

2

International Lending and Risk Assessment

The international debt crisis of the 1980s has heightened the perceived need among international bankers for better country risk analysis. As Irving S. Friedman, one of the originators of formal country risk analysis by banks, recently observed, "More and more bankers believe that a practical, efficient country risk system is essential."[1] Friedman's comments are true for major money center and regional banks. For example, Gerald J. Alifano, a former executive vice president at Pittsburgh National, in drawing "some lessons for the future" from the debt crisis of the 1980s, wrote that "events have reconfirmed the necessity of implementing a risk/reward threshold for an individual market. If the cost of maintaining an on-the-spot presence in a country, or at least, a full-time political-economist, cannot be justified, you're better off staying out."[2]

The growing need for country analysis, moreover, extends to both short-term and long-term lending. Even trade financing can be adversely affected by country risk events. One of Alifano's "lessons" is that "short-term trade financing will never be rescheduled. That myth has certainly been blown out of the water. Short-term lending, including deposit placements, have become an integral part of country debt renegotiation."[3] Daniel R. Denison, a vice president at First Interstate Bank of California, essentially agrees:

> Some banks have eschewed direct term lending altogether but do provide short-term export financing for their customers and maintain "due from" accounts with foreign correspondents. Country risk analysis is important for these banks as well as those active in long-term lending. When a country approaches default, its currency becomes non-convertible. Short-term creditors (even overnight creditors) can suffer along with long-term creditors.[4]

The need for good country risk analysis, therefore, transcends different sizes of international banks and types of loans.

COUNTRY RISK ASSESSMENT APPROACHES

The predominant country risk approach among U.S. banks has evolved. From an unstructured qualitative, informal system in the pre–1973 period, most major banks established formal, structured qualitative systems soon after the first oil shock. The first formal system, which was developed at Citibank by Friedman, is a good example of a mid–1970s structured qualitative method. Since this system was still in place in the 1980s, a detailed description of the Citibank approach to country risk is appropriate.

The structured aspects of the system at Citibank pertain mostly to the managerial decision-making process and do not imply a standardized conceptual model for risk analysis. Citibank does list variables that a country risk report will typically address, but since there are no precise interrelationships posited between the variables, particularly the sociopolitical and macroeconomic, they form more or less a laundry list of factors to consider. Friedman recently described these variables.

> Citicorp monitored country conditions and other elements needed for country assessments and judgments and compiled, if necessary, a large variety of statistical indicators of national creditworthiness. It analyzed domestic economic conditions, outlook, and policies; balance of payments and management thereof; other international economic and financial aspects; principal economic sectors—trends and prospects, flow of funds, and financial intermediation—actual and potential. Other factors included political conditions and outlook; social conditions; international positions and relations; and impact of world events—economic, political, and military. All these factors were brought together and joined into a single comprehensive country risk assessment.[5]

In contrast to how assessments are reached, the managerial process for making final country risk decisions was very precise and fully defined. In fact, the emphasis at Citibank has been to create a country risk management culture that would permeate the entire organization, fostered by a highly standardized process that emphasizes input from the field. For example, country exposure limits or ceilings were established every year in conjunction with the annual budget process. New country ceilings were recommended each year by the senior officer in each country and justified with an accompanying "Country Risk Review," basically a narrative report. After conferring with the regional head in New York, Friedman, as head of country risk, would review the recommendations for final approval; he was aided, of course, by staff reports and external contacts. Strict controls were put in place to insure that this system was not circumvented.[6]

In addition to standard operating procedures, Bankers Trust has developed a structured qualitative model of analysis. It essentially has three major components: the country's environment (with subcomponents being internal political environment, resource endowment, and external environment), the political goals and economic policy/strategy of the government, and economic performance.

The internal political environment is measured by assessing the leadership's ideology, integrity and support base, opposition groups, culture, and the role of the military, which are seen as shaping the formation of political goals. The country's resource endowment (capital, technology, workforce, etc.) and external environment (oil prices, interest rates, trade trends, inflation, OECD growth) together yield external constraints on economic policy. These constraints come together with political goals to form a government's development strategy and economic policies, which have an economic performance outcome. Performance then has a strong feedback effect on economic strategy and policy and a weak impact on environmental factors.

This model leads to a classification scheme called stages of the policy cycle. In stage one economic equilibrium is present when: political goals fit economic constraints, economic policy is consistently formulated, external shocks are absent or managed effectively, and economic performance is reinforcing political goals. In stage two, however, signs of disequilibrium set in, such as an external shock occurring or when there is an inconsistent formulation of economic policy or a misfit of goals to economic constraints. Stage three is a "balance-of-payments crisis," which is caused by: a very strong external shock, continued conflict between goals and economic constraints, or the failure to implement appropriate economic policies. Stage four, on the other hand, involves rescheduling and recovery, when fundamental economic policy changes are implemented because of strong external pressures. These categories guide the timing and intensity of country risk evaluations at the bank.[7]

The Bankers Trust model, a very significant step in the systematic integration of sociopolitical and macroeconomic variables, was developed after the bank upgraded political factors within their country risk assessments in the late 1970s. The notion that there is an observable interaction between a country's given environment and its political goals and economic policy, strategy, and performance is an important analytical point that facilitates integration of data and leads to a useful classification scheme.

Few of the many banks that utilized a structured qualitative approach in the mid–1970s attempted to develop models as precise and comprehensive as that of Bankers Trust. Most major banks instead turned to checklist systems during the late 1970s and 1980s, and still use them.[8] One good example of a checklist system, shown in Table 6, is the one used at American Express. Deciding final scores for each country is a qualitative exercise, and countries are then classified into A-to-E risk rankings. The major advantage of this kind of system is the ease of making comparisons between countries.[9]

An unusual example of a checklist approach, shown in Table 7, is one that does not include any sociopolitical variables. As an international economist at Mellon Bank explained, "Political and social variables are missing, not because such factors are unimportant but because they are not quantifiable and can be obtained only through detailed country analysis."[10]

Mellon's country evaluation system highlights a major flaw in the checklist

Table 6
Country Scoring System at American Express

Country Variables	Score/Weight
Extent of foreign capital dependence	15
Import dependence	10
Vulnerability of revenues	15
Debt servicing burden	15
Monetary and fiscal control	15
Hospitality to private and foreign capital	5
Comparative importance of country	5
Political risk	20
	100

Source: Emilio Mayer, International Lending: Country Risk Analysis (Reston: Reston Financial Services, 1985), p. 72.

approach: a predetermined weighting system, by its very nature distorts or ignores certain available and perhaps important information. David Lomax, Group Economic Advisor at National Westminster Bank, made the same point.

> The vast majority of [country risk] systems . . . consists of setting up a kind of beauty competition in which factors such as debt service ratio, growth, ratio of debt to exports and to GNP, qualitative factors like membership of the EEC, the level of resources, are given marks. These are often added up to form a score, which is then used to select the prettiest girl in the class or the most ugly. . . . A major problem . . . is that they deliberately discard what might be relevant information, or give it an inappropriate weight. . . . There is a deliberate policy of not collecting together all the information which may be relevant, and of not weighting it or valuing it according to the particular circumstances.[11]

Another major disadvantage of the checklist approach is the unreasonable assumption that the same factor or variable has the same impact in every country. James Merrill, a senior vice president at Marine Midland, made this observation:

Table 7
Country Evaluation System at Mellon Bank

Variables	Score/Weight
Liquidity	
Reserves to imports	40
Debt service to exports	20
Large reserve losses	10
Late payment experience	10
IMF credit to quota	20
	100
Structural Analysis	
% change in consumer prices	10
% change in M, to % change real GNP	10
Change in domestic credit, monetary base	10
Purchasing power parity	10
Country export growth to world export growth	30
Exports of goods and services to GDP	10
Total debt to exports of goods and services	15
Savings to GDP	10
Growth real per capita	5
	100

Source: Emilio Mayer, Interntional Lending: Country Risk Analysis (Reston: Reston Financial Services, 1985), pp. 69-70.

A limitation of this method [checklists] is that each factor is treated as equally important in every country, whereas we know that inflation or labor strikes affect different countries in different ways. Furthermore, conditions may change because they are persistently unstable, or a fundamental change may take place that is relatively permanent.[12]

An excellent example of Merrill's last point is represented by the Shah's Iran. Up until the eve of the revolution, Iran would have been rated as being highly creditworthy by all known checklist systems because of strong economic indicators, regardless of the score given to political risk. Checklist systems can downplay certain factors that at a particular point in time have an overriding impact on country risk.

Chemical Bank, perhaps recognizing many of these deficiencies, has developed a checklist system that is much different from those typically used at other banks. Relative weighting for Chemical Bank's four major areas of analysis—economic, political, external debt management, and confidence—can be different for each country, depending entirely on managerial judgment. A score of 1–9 is given for each of these four areas. Total points per area are then used to classify countries into nine categories of risk.

The Chemical Bank system obviously avoids the major drawbacks of the typical checklist system.[13] The bank's approach does not assume each factor has the same impact in all countries, and it accepts the possibility that one factor may have an overriding importance in a country at a certain time. Chemical Bank also avoids the tendency of checklist systems to become too focused on a few variables. Economic and external debt management scores are determined by in-depth, comprehensive analysis of macroeconomic data. Projections at least four years into the future are emphasized. For politics, a political spread sheet method is used, essentially O'Leary and Coplin's "Prince Model." A narrative report prompted by formatted questions justifies all the numerical ratings.

The avoidance of the main drawbacks of the typical checklist system, however, are obtained at the expense of increased dependence on subjective analysis or opinion. Determining final weights and scores for each area is largely unstructured and highly qualitative. Unlike the Bankers Trust model, ranking is done by subjective, numerical ratings that are not based on observable relationships between sociopolitical and macroeconomic variables. The Chemical Bank approach keeps economics and politics separate, except for comparing scores between the two. The interaction of politics and economics is not intrinsic to the system, as it is in the Bankers Trust model.

At the Bank of America, an attempt is made to avoid the strong subjective, qualitative character of all previously discussed approaches. The bank employs a computer-assisted system that combines an analytical formula with judgments to produce an overall country risk rating. The first and most basic step in their system is the quantitative, statistical examination of a country, leading to the formation of a debt-service capacity index. In essence this index had two subindices: the debt service index (debt service capacity ratios, import coverage, debt burden, and import compressibility) and the adaptability index (gross domestic product, inflation, exports, product concentration, and saving patterns). By a statistical estimation procedure, economic conditions of a country in a base year are correlated with the debt-servicing record of the country for the next one to five years. It was discovered that liquidity or the debt service index was the best statistical predictor of a country's short-term ability to repay its debt on time, whereas structural economic variables (the adaptability index) were more important for the long run (five years). A balanced composite of debt service and adaptability indices was the best predictor for the medium term of three years. Thus the debt service capacity index was formed.

After basic quantitative analysis, judgmental factors are considered, as listed in Table 8. Ratings for these factors are made initially by country and regional managers in a questionnaire format, and the responses are sent to divisional headquarters, where preliminary ratings are given to each country. Final ratings, which rank risk on a scale from A to F, are made at corporate headquarters and reviewed by top management. Traditionally, judgmental indicators have been secondary in importance to the quantitative analysis, but recently have received increased emphasis.[14]

The history of country risk analysis at Bank of America reflects the drawbacks of being too dependent on statistical models when doing country risk assessments. As Merrill at Marine Midland argued, "this method [econometrics] has the disadvantage that it deals only with economic data. That relationships that are true on average for many countries are used to predict individual country results, and that the statistical significance is not as high as might be desired."[15] Such disadvantages, moreover, are fairly well recognized, and as a result, Krishan Saini and Philip Bates recently reported that "no institution lending money to developing countries is placing exclusive reliance on a statistical model to guide its actions."[16] This observation is certainly true for Bank of America over time.

Thus, the predominant approach to country risk assessment varies from bank to bank and covers the gamut of methodological options. Although checklist systems still appear to be the most widely used approach, bankers increasingly have raised questions about their accuracy. In addition few banks either rely heavily on econometric models or leave country risk analysis to informal, unstructured decision making. The critical issue for many if not most major banks is how best to structure both the qualitative and quantitative analysis of a country—and that question remains largely unanswered. As Paul Sachs commented,

> No bank has achieved a significant breakthrough in the way it evaluates sovereign creditworthiness which might compel other institutions to follow suit. Sovereign risk analysis remains an art, not a science. Technical restraints continue to impede any consensus; no one has yet figured out how to accurately predict all the various elements of risk inherent in sovereign lending. As we enter the 1980s, variety continued as the rule.[17]

COUNTRY RISK MANAGEMENT SYSTEMS

A country risk management system is the process by which country exposure limits are determined. Country risk assessments are only one part of that process.

Table 8
Judgmental Indicators at Bank of America

Economic Indicators

- effectiveness of monetary policy
- government's fiscal policy
- financial regulatory policies
- government attitude toward investment
- quality of management
- access to international credit
- exchange rate policy

Political Indicators

- government's effectiveness in formulating coherent policies
- conflict resolution capacity of government institutions
- orderly succession of government
- degree of checks and balances within government institutions
- potential for social unrest
- potential external security threats
- relations with United States
- relevant regional alliances

Source: Emilio Mayer, International Lending: Country Risk Analysis (Reston: Reston Financial Services, 1985), pp. 75-76.

How assessments are used to set loan ceilings by country and by type of loan is perhaps the most crucial step in the country risk management process.

The predominant approach to country risk management in the 1970s was the line-driven system, in which the country manager is the main actor. This arrangement matched the lending bias of the times, when markets were flat in the

United States and the problem of recycling petrodollars called for an aggressive lending stance. At the present time, however, most major banks are not line-driven in their country risk management procedures, and both the credit and staff functions have become more important.

The four major money center banks whose approaches to country risk assessment have been presented here—Citibank, Chemical Bank, Bankers Trust, and Bank of America—also represent a good spectrum of the country risk management systems now in place. Citibank still employs a line-driven system in which country risk evaluations and loan proposals start with the senior officer in a country. The country manager's recommendation is routed through a variety of regional and area managers who can modify or amend it. The evaluation and proposal finally reaches a senior vice president, who has the title Senior Adviser for International Operations, for final approval of country exposure limits. Although this senior manager often solicits staff reports and external expertise and then forms ad hoc country risk meetings, the final decision remains focused in one office, the senior manager's. Friedman, the first manager in that position, had this comment:

> At Citibank, the focus of country risk decision making was the world headquarters. Frequent exchanges of ideas and information between field officers and headquarters were seen as vitally important and encouraged. As time went on and experience gained, the whole process became more and more field-driven. Field resistance to the burden of country assessment and reporting declined as the process proved useful in enabling the field to expand business and earnings . . . without excessive risk.[18]

Many other banks, however, have established decision-making mechanisms that serve to check the loan biases of line managers. The way this is done varies widely, but Sachs, after surveying eight money center banks, found three basic types of systems: primarily line, parallel stream, and duplicate stream. Of the eight banks surveyed in 1983, only one was classified as primarily line.[19]

Five of the banks were categorized as having parallel stream approaches, in which line managers and headquarters staff submit separate assessments and recommendations, with little interaction between staff and line. Conflicts between staff and line are usually resolved by the senior credit officer.

Chemical Bank follows this pattern. Detailed marketing reports, which include a loan exposure proposal, are prepared by the lending side of the bank. Juxtaposed against this process, the Country Risk Management Group of the Credit Division completes at least an annual evaluation of each country where Chemical Bank has or is contemplating cross-border exposure, and proposes an exposure limit. Both the marketing report prepared by the line and the country risk evaluation submitted by staff go to the Country Risk Management Committee, which is chaired by the bank's chief credit officer. The committee, which meets monthly, makes final decisions regarding country risk ratings and exposure limits. Although decisions are formally taken by majority vote, the chairman of the committee has great informal power and quite a bit of influence on final outcomes; the chief credit officer can alone approve loans beyond exposure limits and can make country risk decisions between committee meetings.

The other two banks examined here, Bankers Trust and the Bank of America, use duplicate stream systems, in which staff and line prepare separate country risk reports after considerable interaction. At Bankers Trust, for example, line managers propose country exposure limits after extensive discussions with the Economics Department. Although these proposals are, of course, supported by country risk evaluations, line evaluations tend to focus on economic variables, even if political considerations are often mentioned. Political factors receive considerably more emphasis at the staff level. A four-member Political Assessment Group reports through the chief international economist to the two executive vice presidents involved in international business and to the bank's chief credit officer. During country risk reviews, an annual process chaired by the chief international economist, two separate reports by staff and line are presented and discussed. As these reviews take place, the Country Risk Committee also meets and sets exposure limits. The committee is composed of the two executive vice presidents mentioned above and the chief credit officer. Although disputes that arise on the committee are formally settled by majority vote, the decision is often delegated to a senior vice president in charge of the International Department's risk management.

The Bank of America also has what can be generally described as a duplicate stream system, but the details of its country risk management process differ dramatically from Bankers Trust. Ideally, country risk ratings, which form the basis for exposure limits, are set by consensus between the Economics Department at headquarters and line management. The Country Risk Evaluation Advisory Committee, consisting of the bank's senior credit officer and chief economists from each of its regional divisions, reviews the ratings if consensus is reached. Such consensus, however, is infrequent, and country rating decisions are often settled by the World Banking Executive Council, composed of the executive vice presidents in credit and administration. These senior managers have no stake in the marketing of loans and have extensive international experience. The Council also sets country exposure limits in all instances.

As with country risk assessment, the approach taken to set exposure limits varies greatly among major U.S. banks. Briance Mascarenhas and Ole Christian Sand, using a classification scheme that differs from the one employed by Sachs, nevertheless found similar diversity. Twenty-one banks in Mascarenhas' and Sand's fifty-bank sample exhibited an essentially line-driven approach to country risk management. Twenty-nine banks, however, exhibited characteristics that were similar to Sachs' duplicate and parallel stream systems, with a formal country risk assessment unit at the corporate level and a country limit committee that received reports from both the corporate assessment unit and individual country managers.[20]

In spite of this diversity in country risk management systems, the surveys indicate a general trend of staff and credit managers gaining substantially more influence, perhaps reflecting a growing conservatism and sophistication in international lending. Certainly the vesting of final authority to set country exposure limits in the chief credit officer or in a committee largely controlled by that officer fits the circumstances of the post–1982 lending environment. Given higher country risks and the continued presence of attractive international lending opportunities, it seems appropriate that U.S. banks are devoting more resources, and giving greater importance to country risk evaluations prepared by staff.

SOURCES OF COUNTRY RISK INFORMATION

U.S. banks depend on a variety of sources when collecting country risk information. Although the relative importance of different sources seems to change with new circumstances and experiences, particularly with those as traumatic as the Iranian revolution and the 1982 debt crisis, some sources have been used fairly consistently, as Table 9 suggests.

Other banks and headquarters personnel were mentioned as basic sources of country risk information by at least 75 percent of major U.S. banks surveyed in 1981 and 1983 (samples of eleven and eighteen banks respectively).[21] At the same time, consultants, agents, and outside counsel were used by less than half of all bank respondents in both periods. Interestingly, U.S. government agencies and international organizations were rated by significantly fewer banks as a basic source of country risk information in 1983 versus 1981. Sample bias does not adequately explain this change, since many of the same banks were in the two surveys and both studies were conducted by the same researcher. Perhaps a reduction in the use of the U.S. government as a source of country risk information reflects a growing lack of confidence in the validity of such information within the business community since the Iranian revolution. A similar loss of confidence in international organizations, like the International Monetary Fund, could be seen as flowing from some banks' disillusionment with the IMF's ''strong arm'' management of the international debt crisis of the 1980s.[22]

Business periodicals, affiliate managers, the public media (newspapers, television, radio), and host government managers, on the other hand, were elevated in relative importance between the 1981 and 1983 studies. Such a trend reinforces a finding reported earlier that most banks have increased their resources devoted to country risk analysis since 1982. The rise in the use of business periodicals and the public media follows the heightened activity of corporate staff in the country assessment process, whereas the increased reliance on affiliate and host government managers reflects the realization that independent, grass-roots intelligence collection is an essential counterweight to external sources of information if the firm is to take country risk analysis seriously.

Table 9
Sources of Country Risk Information as a Percentage of U.S. Bank Respondents Citing Source

	75% or Over		50-74%		Under 50%	
	1981	1983	1981	1983	1981	1983
Other Banks	X	X				
U.S. Government Agencies	X			X		
Headquarters Personnel	X	X				
International Organizations	X			X		
Business Periodicals		X	X			
Affiliate Managers		X	X			
Public Media		X	X			
Agents and Outside Counsel					X	X
Consultants					X	X
Local (Host) Government Managers				X	X	

Source: Robert Grosse and John Stock, "Noneconomic Risk Evaluation in Multinational Banks," Management International Review, January 1984, p. 50; and Robert Grosse, "Political Risk Evaluation Procedures Used in U.S.-Based Banks," Political Risks in International Business: New Directions for Research, Management and Public Policy, Thomas Brewer, ed. (New York: Praeger Publishers, 1985), p. 245.

BANKER PERCEPTIONS OF COUNTRY RISK

In a recent survey, twenty-nine banks were asked to rate the importance of various country risk variables.[23] Each variable was rated as receiving high, low or no priority, as Table 10 shows.

A number of observations are suggested by the data. The high importance attached to the state of the country's external accounts has been traditional to the banking community for obvious reasons; banks are mainly interested in a country's capacity to generate foreign exchange in order to service its external debt, and balance-of-payment entries are the best objective measure of such capacity. Capacity to service debt is also the key consideration that explains the relatively high priority assigned to variables measuring the structure of exports.

Apart from the capacity to service debt, the country should have the willingness to meet its debt obligations as well. The two variables that most directly measure

Table 10
Perceptions of Country Risk Variables by Banks as a Percent of Bank Respondents

	High Priority	Low or No Priority
Current Account Balance	100	0
Trade Balance	93	7
Balance of Payments	93	7
GNP Growth Rate	90	10
Diversity and Stability of Exports	86	14
Market Concentration of Exports	82	18
Inflation	79	21
Foreign Exchange Controls	76	24
Foreign Exchange Rate	68	32
Money Supply Growth Rate	63	37
Savings as % GNP	59	41
GNP Per Capita	55	45
Investment as % GNP	52	48
Foreign Investment Climate	52	48
Terms of Trade	45	55
Labor Force Profile	37	63
Interest Rates	28	72

Source: R. Peter DeWitt and Jeff Madura, "How Banks Assess County Risk: A Survey," University of Central Florida, unpublished manuscript, pp. 3-8.

the will to pay are foreign exchange controls and foreign investment climate. The survey results may be interpreted to suggest that regulatory policy decisions, like foreign exchange controls, are rated more important than general societal attitudes or political instability potential, since these considerations presumably

Table 11
Managerial Perceptions of Political versus Economic Criteria in Country Risk

Criteria	Average Ranking, Sovereign Loans	Average Ranking, Corporate Loans
Credit History	2.32	1.81
Financial Factors	2.00	2.89
Political Factors	1.50	1.22

Source: R. Peter DeWitt and Jeff Madura, "How Banks Assess Country Risk: A Survey," University of Central Florida, unpublished manuscript, p. 9.

are contained within the investment climate variable. This ranking may reflect a general bias against pure political risk factors; note that the only other political risk factor on the list, labor force profile, is also rated low in priority. The ranking may also mirror the fact that legal-governmental risk events cause more financial losses than extra-legal incidents, particularly when applied to the banking community since the 1982 debt crisis. In general, however, political factors receive far less weight and attention than do economic criteria. For example, twenty-nine major banks recently indicated that financial factors and credit history far outweighed political risk considerations when making sovereign and corporate loans abroad, as Table 11 demonstrates.

These rankings may or may not conform to actual outcomes and past experiences regarding nonpayment or rescheduling of debt. No one has scientifically determined the precise causal relationships associated with the financial losses incurred by the international banking community. Nevertheless, the elevation of political factors in relative importance will occur within banks only when a systematic and comprehensive model of country risk is developed. Without such a model, bankers are generally at a loss as to how to integrate obviously important political factors with the financial considerations that they have traditionally stressed.

NOTES

1. Irving S. Friedman, *The World Debt Dilemma: Managing Country Risk* (Philadelphia: Council for International Banking Studies, 1983), p. 281.
2. Gerald J. Alifano, "A Reassessment of International Banking: A Regional Bank Point of View," *The Journal of Commercial Bank Lending*, January 1984, p. 13.
3. Ibid., p. 12.

4. Daniel R. Denison, "A Pragmatic Model for Country Risk Analysis," *The Journal of Commercial Bank Lending*, March 1984, p. 30.

5. Friedman, *World Debt Dilemma*, p. 256.

6. Ibid., pp. 251–67.

7. Lawrence J. Brainard, "Bankers Trust's Approach to International Risk Assessment," *Assessing Country Risk*, Richard Ensor, ed. (London: Euromoney Publications, 1981), pp. 93–98.

8. Robert Grosse, "Political Risk Evaluation Procedures Used in U.S.-Based Banks," *Political Risks in International Business: New Directions for Research, Management, and Public Policy*, Thomas Brewer, ed. (New York: Praeger Publishers, 1985), p. 244.

9. Tim Anderson, "More Models than Vogue Magazine," *Euromoney*, November 1982, p. 45.

10. Emilio Mayer, *International Lending: Country Risk Analysis* (Reston: Reston Financial Services, 1985), p. 70.

11. David Lomax, "Sovereign Risk Analysis Now," *The Banker*, January 1983, p. 35.

12. James Merrill, "Country Risk Analysis," *Columbia Journal of World Business*, Spring 1982, p. 90.

13. For a discussion of country risk from the perspective of a vice president of Chemical Bank, see Joseph Tunney, "Bank Perspectives in Measuring Risk," *Assessing Country Risk*, Richard Ensor, ed. (London: Euromoney Publications, 1981), pp. 83–86.

14. Friedman, *World Debt Dilemma*, p. 270.

15. Merrill, "Country Risk Analysis," p. 89.

16. Krishan Saini and Philip Bates, "A Survey of the Quantitative Approaches to Country Risk Analysis," *Journal of Banking and Finance*, June 1984, p. 353.

17. Paul Sachs, "Setting Country Limits: Approaches of Major U.S. Banks," *International Political Risk Management: New Dimensions*, Fariborz Ghadar and Theodore Moran, eds. (Washington, D.C.: Ghadar and Associates, 1984), p. 35.

18. Friedman, *World Debt Dilemma*, p. 253.

19. Sachs, "Setting Country Limits," p. 40.

20. Briance Mascarenhas and Ole Christian Sand, "Country-Risk Assessment Systems in Banks: Patterns and Performance," *Journal of International Business Studies*, Spring 1985, pp. 23–27.

21. Grosse, "Political Risk Evaluation," p. 245; and Robert Grosse and John Stack, "Noneconomic Risk Evaluation in Multinational Banks," *Management International Review*, January 1984, p. 50.

22. The most notorious and the first major incident of "arm-twisting" by the IMF against commercial banks occurred in November 1982 during IMF negotiations concerning a rescue package for Mexico.

23. R. Peter DeWitt and Jeff Madura, "How Banks Assess Country Risk: A Survey," University of Central Florida, unpublished manuscript, pp. 3–8.

3

Country Risk Management

In attempting to chart new directions in country risk management, one should first make explicit certain fundamental assumptions. The most basic assumption is that political and economic factors are highly and dynamically interrelated. Their degree of interaction is so great as to require incorporation of both sets of variables into a single conceptual model. Their interaction is also very dynamic; the relative importance of different variables changes often within a country and among countries. As a result, in-depth country analysis is continually required. As Friedman commented, "There is simply no labor-saving device yet invented that can spare us the effort of painstakingly examining each country individually."[1] Of course, one should frame such examination through the lens of a systematic and integrated model.

A model as a set of precisely defined, measured, and integrated variables is a simplified theoretical representation of the real world. As stated earlier, the scientific identification of the most relevant variables and their interrelationships in the area of country risk has not been fully accomplished. Without those variables and interrelationships, a model in the true sense of the word cannot be built. As a first step in model building, then, a conceptual framework can be erected: a schema of explicitly defined and interrelated variables. The most relevant variables and relationships can be reasonably posited and supported by both deductive logic and empirical evidence. The resulting conceptual framework can serve as a critical building block in the theorizing process. Research, outside the scope of this book, could then fully explore the relevance and precision of the variables and their relationships. Until such efforts lead to formal model building, researchers and managers need guidance, and a conceptual framework of explicitly defined relationships can provide a directional compass of sorts that both professions can use in their subsequent work.

A POLITICAL ECONOMY FRAMEWORK FOR COUNTRY RISK

The chief purpose of erecting a conceptual framework of political economy is to provide a structure for managers so that they can do more systematic and rigorous analysis. By identifying relevant variables and their interrelationships, a conceptual framework allows managers to focus on the major issues and questions. As David Lomax commented, "The [main] issue is more one of posing the right question to ensure that the information is processed and assessed in the correct manner."[2]

The conceptual framework presented here could be best described as a structured qualitative approach. As shown in Figure 5, it incorporates and interrelates qualitative sociopolitical factors with quantitative economic data.[3] Political economy itself is based on the premise that the most relevant economic decisions—which for our purposes include those that most strongly impact international lending prospects—are made through a political process. These key political and economic decisions can be characterized as country strategy, having two components: most fundamentally, strategic goals or objectives are chosen and are largely shaped by the domestic and international context; then, macroeconomic policies are enacted and implemented to achieve these goals, which have an economic performance outcome. Broad relationships between country strategy, context, and performance thus become crucial elements in country risk analysis.

As the sizes of the arrows in Figure 5 imply, the strength of causality between these three elements differs. The context has a strong influence on country strategy, while the context is relatively given and largely uncontrollable in the short term by the political process. Of course, macroeconomic policies produced by the political process have a large and fairly immediate impact on economic performance, which in turn has an effect, albeit a weaker impact, on country strategy and the context. Lastly, the context can have an influence on economic performance, equal to that of strategy or policy.

This framework of political economy is an alternative to the three other basic country risk methodologies: fully qualitative, checklist, and econometric. The first alternative is clearly inferior to the model of political economy. Without any structure or standardized format, there can be little systematic and disciplined analysis.

Checklist systems, the most popular country risk approach by U.S. banks, are flawed in a number of ways. Most fundamentally, structural shifts, either economic or political, are outside the purview of checklist or weighting systems. For example, any known checklist system in use now or at the time of the Iranian revolution would have failed to rate that country a high credit risk. By giving variables predetermined weights, checklist systems can downplay overriding and deterministic forces which may emerge in a particular context. Some important variables may not be addressed or weighted at all. Thus by their nature, checklist and weighting systems distort or ignore much of the available information. But

Figure 5
A Political Economy Framework

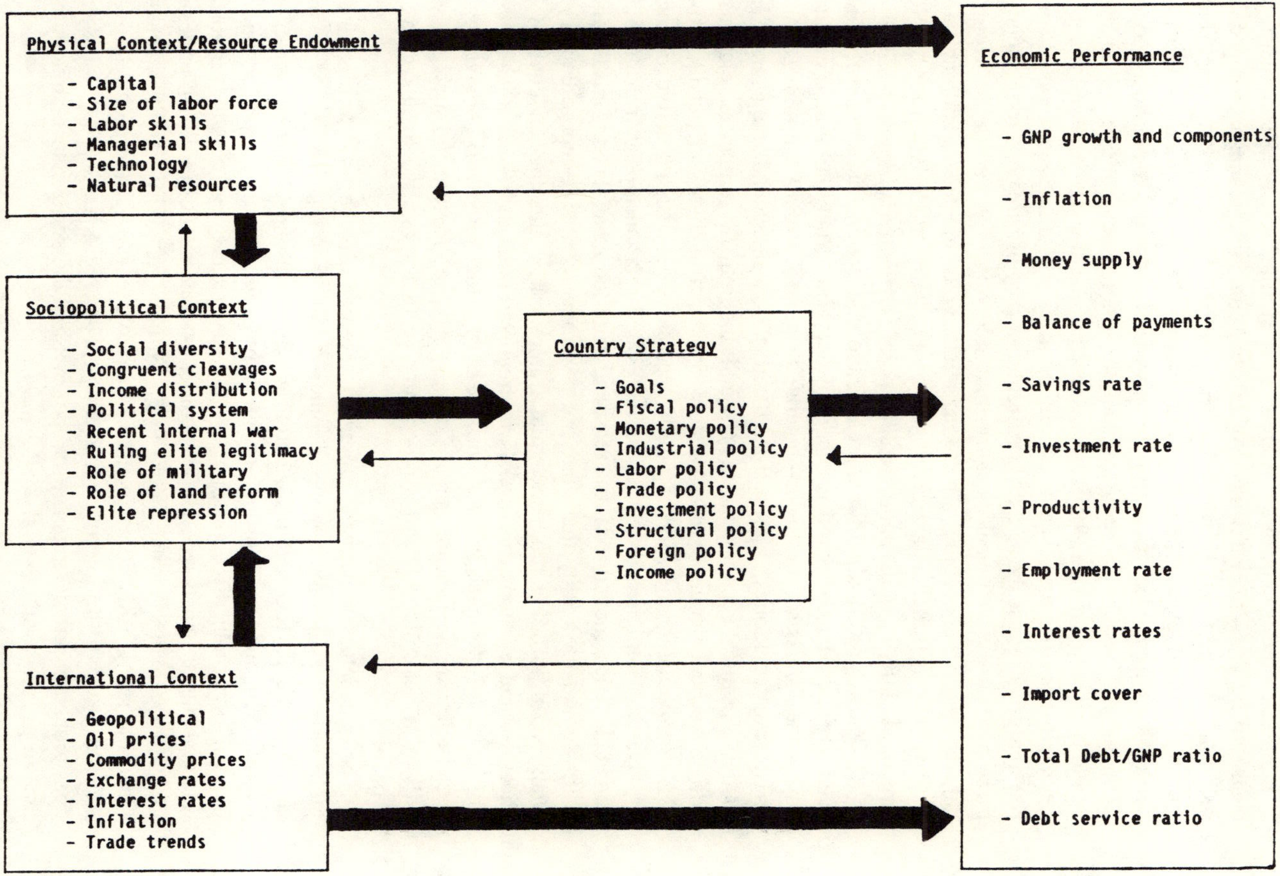

perhaps their most important weakness is that they tend to encourage mechanistic decision making, which is a profoundly antimanagerial habit.

Econometric models can be dangerous for similar reasons. Econometric forecasts can be one important piece of information for a manager doing country risk analysis, particularly for short-term lending decisions, but these kinds of forecasts can never be relied on as sole sources. Long-term lending decisions in particular require a more strategic analysis of a country's political economy. Econometric models, moreover, generally ignore sociopolitical variables and would have utterly failed, for example, to send warning signals about Iran before 1978. Econometric models are also limited in their usefulness as tools of country risk analysis because the statistical correlations they use are not strong. Relatedly, these models are also weak because their selection of variables has been more data driven than conceptual, due to the relative incompleteness and unreliability of hard international data. Lastly, an econometric model's ability to predict structural shifts in the economy and in policy are extremely low.

As a structured qualitative approach, the conceptual framework of political economy must be compared to others of this type. Many structured qualitative approaches are based on expert-generated opinion, usually through Delphi interviewing techniques. It is assumed here that well trained managers using a model of political economy based on sound, theoretically supported relationships will make better country risk decisions for the firm than will outside experts. The conceptual framework of political economy is also attractive because it provides a comprehensive set of variables and relationships that are explicitly defined and designed to stimulate reasoned and focused analysis. Thus the framework depicts the reality that there are no productive short-cuts to country risk analysis. In so doing this conceptual framework avoids the tendency of both checklist and econometric models to treat variables as if they had the same impact and importance in all countries. Lastly, the framework is advantageous because it facilitates an analysis of a country's basic structure and strategy, which will be a better long-term, cross-country predictor relative to alternative approaches.

The conceptual framework presented here can also be used to erect a comprehensive classification scheme of countries as to their relative state of riskiness, shown in Table 12. In general countries can be grouped into five categories: political-economic equilibrium, or either possible, minor, major, or traumatic political-economic disequilibrium. Within each category, certain variables or relationships are analyzed. These include: external shocks (e.g., oil prices) and their management; internal shocks (e.g., political instability) and their management; the relationship between strategy and context (e.g., the policy impact on specific groups); the internal consistency of strategic goals and policies (e.g., does monetary policy support fiscal policy); and the performance-strategy interface (e.g., are strategic goals being met).

It is important to note three idiosyncrasies in this classification scheme. First, it contains an inherently conservative bias, so that if any one condition in the

Table 12
States of Country Riskiness

1. Political-Economic Equilibrium

   a. economic performance is meeting major goals <u>and</u>
   b. strategic goals and policies fit the context <u>and</u>
   c. strategic goals and policies are internally consistent <u>and</u>
   d. external disequilibrium is absent or managed effectively <u>and</u>
   e. political instability potential is relatively low

2. Possible Political-Economic Disequilibrium

   a. adverse economic performance is predicted <u>or</u>
   b. strategic goals and policies do not fit the context <u>or</u>
   c. an adverse economic policy shift is predicted <u>or</u>
   d. external shock is predicted <u>or</u>
   e. political instability potential is relatively moderate

3. Minor Political-Economic Disequilibrium

   a. economic performance drops or fails to meet goals <u>or</u>
   b. goals, policies and/or performance is causing the context to adversely change <u>or</u>
   c. strategic goals and policies are internally inconsistent <u>or</u>
   d. external shock has occurred <u>or</u>
   e. political instability potential is relatively high

4. Major Political-Economic Disequilibrium

   a. there exists an economic performance crisis <u>or</u>
   b. serious policy mismanagement is present <u>or</u>
   c. external shock has a strong adverse impact <u>or</u>
   d. political violence and/or disruptions are high

5. Traumatic Political-Economic Disequilibrium

   a. there has been an economic collapse <u>or</u>
   b. the policy process has collapsed <u>or</u>
   c. external shock has an overriding and adverse impact <u>or</u>
   d. political instability or chaos is present

most serious category of riskiness holds, then the country is classified in that category. Such a bias perhaps fits the present international business atmosphere. Second, there are multiple layers of country risk types within each of the four disequilibrium categories. For example, a set of countries may all be in minor disequilibrium, but one country may have three of the conditions for such a state of disequilibrium, while the other countries have only one or two conditions. Generally speaking, the country with three of the conditions is a more risky lending opportunity relative to the others. Third, turnaround cases or countries are implicit within each of the three most serious categories of riskiness. Two countries may be in major disequilibrium, but if one is significantly improving its political economy, then that country is less risky than the other case, where the situation may seem to be stagnating or even deteriorating.

Although the conceptual framework and classification scheme just described is similar to the approach used at Bankers Trust, the political economy framework of country risk has a number of distinctive advantages. First, the Bankers Trust approach depicts the formation of political goals as taking place independent of the country's resource base or external environment, a highly questionable premise. As one banker insisted, the first step in country risk analysis should be analysis of the resource base, because "with the resource base well understood, the appropriateness of a government's economic and financial policies can then be considered."[4]

In a related point the Bankers Trust labeling of the country's goals in political terms, reflecting the deterministic influence of the internal political environment on goal formation, misses the crucial point that countries, like companies, are usually guided by certain overall strategic objectives. A firm's or country's mission is typically formulated as a result of a private or public manager's assessment of the organization's strengths and weaknesses internally and externally. Thus when a bank does country risk analysis, the entire range of contextual conditions (physical, sociopolitical, and international) should be brought together and juxtaposed against the government's policy capabilities to derive a strategic mission for the country.

The political economy framework of country risk is also theoretically based, in that its sociopolitical variables are drawn explicitly from empirical research on mass political violence. Variables used at Bankers Trust are similar to those used here but are not as precise or as comprehensive.

In addition relationships that exist among the major categories of analysis (context, strategy, and performance) within the Bankers Trust model are weakly or incompletely developed. The performance of the economy is seen as solely the result of economic policy and development strategy. Obviously, the country's context can have a major and direct impact on performance, independent of the government's policies.

Regardless of these comparisons, the major flaw in the Bankers Trust approach actually lies not within the conceptual model itself but within the classification scheme derived from the model. The notion that countries go through a policy cycle or through certain identifiable progressive stages of riskiness is particularly flawed because it misses certain dynamics of the development process. Countries can and often do jump from one developmental condition to another. There is rarely a natural flow from one stage to the next logical one within a cycle or sequence. A classification scheme of country riskiness is better served by the notion of independently derived and mutually exclusive categories. This allows for the reality that countries can go from one category to any other without going through intermediate steps. The developing world is a very dynamic and revolutionary one that contradicts the notion of incremental stages of development.

CONCEPTUAL FRAMEWORK APPLICATIONS

The first step recommended by the political economy model of country risk analysis is an assessment of economic performance. This reflects the ultimate importance that balance-of-payments analysis has on international lending prospects. A number of balance-of-payment ratios stand out in importance as a basic credit check on a country. One key variable to analyze is aptly called the debt-service ratio; the benchmark standard for annual long-term debt principal and interest payments plus short-term debt interest payments, divided by the country's exports of goods and services, is traditionally 20 percent. Short-term debt amortization is omitted because of the assumption that principal payments in trade-related finance are rolled over when they become due. This ratio is considered in the precautionary zone when it is between 20 and 30 percent; over 30 percent is considered dangerous.

One needs to be cautious, however, when using such ratios, for final country risk decisions should never be made on this basis alone, as the examples of Zaire and Brazil in 1977 well demonstrate. Both countries had debt-service ratios of around 40 percent, well into the danger zone, but that figure meant a far different thing when applied to Zaire than it did in Brazil's case. Zaire was an economy very heavily dependent on few export commodities, while Brazil had a much more diversified and less vulnerable export base. The more assured a country's export earnings—usually measured by product and market diversification—the higher the debt-service ratio can go before there is cause for alarm. Many analysts, in fact, considered Brazil's debt-service ratio in the 1970s to be within an acceptable zone considering the country's structure of exports.

When one looks at debt-service ratios, one is doing structural balance-of-payments analysis. Within such analysis, one should also study both import compressibility, calculated by the percentage of total imports devoted to essential goods, particularly oil and food, and GNP to total external debt ratios. Import compressibility will show a country's capability of reducing imports in a foreign exchange crisis; a figure over 35 percent is considered alarming, and 25–35 percent is precautionary. To go beyond analysis of a country's ability to manage a crisis, comparing GNP to total debt reflects the country's long-term capacity to repay these external obligations; 30–40 percent is considered precautionary, and over 40 percent is regarded as dangerous.

Liquidity balance-of-payments analysis, on the other hand, focuses on cash-flow issues in the near term. The most widely looked at variable is the import-coverage ratio, which measures the length of time a country can import the present volume of imports by drawing down on foreign exchange reserves. The import cover is calculated by dividing imports of goods and services by total reserves and then multiplying that percentage by twelve to get the number of months covered. A coverage ratio of two to three months is considered precautionary, whereas under two is alarming.

Again these numbers and ratios must be approached with care and not be used mechanically as decision-making crutches. Many factors and considerations can raise or lower the acceptable zone or make these ratios irrelevant for any given country at a particular time. The general benchmark standards, however, are useful to know because any unfavorable deviation from the norm should serve as a signal for needed in-depth analysis. As two bankers observed,

> There are quantitative relationships worth looking at in assessing country credit. None can stand alone; each requires to be placed in the context of the country. . . . And all of these indices pale in analytical usefulness when compared to the quality of public sector management.[5]

When one analyzes the economic performance of a country, therefore, a focus on numerical trends alone is misdirected. The role of public-sector management must serve as the lens through which macroeconomic variables are judged. Assessment of economic performance must not be carried out simply in absolute or trend-line terms but in a strategic sense as well. Assessment may need to focus on whether the country's strategic goals are being met. According to Francis Mason, the senior vice president who heads country risk analysis at Chase Manhattan, "What really counts is how the domestic economy is managed, because that eventually will impact the politics. Even more crucial is how the economy is doing against its plans, against its goals."[6]

The example of Brazil in the late 1970s will illustrate this point. Real annual growth in the Brazilian economy began to slow in the late 1970s to the 5–6 percent range, after an average annual real growth rate of 10 percent in the 1971–76 period. One should have not concluded that overall economic performance had dropped, however, for a strategic goal of the Brazilian government since 1977 had been to lower real growth rates in order to slow inflation and improve the country's long-term international competitiveness.

In another example, strategic analysis of Iran's economic performance in 1977 might have given international lenders a warning signal. This is true even though many economic trends in Iran were positive; for example, real GNP grew over 10 percent a year from 1974–77, and international reserves climbed from $8.3 to $12.3 billion. In strategic terms, however, it was questionable whether the Shah was achieving his major objective of rapid and sustained modernization, which would propel Iran to the economic level of Western Europe and Japan by the twenty-first century. By 1977 the successful achievement of such an ambitious objective was becoming less and less possible. With the fall in real oil prices and a skyrocketing budget deficit, the Shah in 1977 was forced to cancel many large development projects. Besides bringing financial savings, the projects that were cancelled would also have lessened the pressure on an already serious problem of huge infrastructure bottlenecks, and inflation might have been moderated from dangerously high levels as well. In effect, 1977 was a year of basic retreat from the previous policy of non-stop, rapid modernization, and this retreat was ushered in by a 1977 change in prime ministers, the first such cabinet move in twelve years.

Given the strategic failure of recent economic performance in the Iran case, a managerial analyst would then have needed to address its cause. The possible causes, besides macroeconomic factors, are: economic policy mismanagement (incompetence, corruption); the country's strategy not fitting the context (goals are unrealistic and policies are adversely changing the context); external shocks (war, oil and commodity prices, interest rates); and/or political instability (riots, civil war, military coups, revolution). In Iran's case the problem was a misfit between strategy and context. The Shah's goals were overly ambitious, and certain policies were causing the domestic sociopolitical context to change dramatically for the worse. The Shah's goal of rapid modernization spawned industrial, investment, and structural policies that had disastrous effects on Iranian society. Most damaging was a land reform program that resulted in massive dislocations within the rural sector, where most of the population was located. As a result, 10 percent of the rural population per year migrated to urban areas in the 1970s, quickly adding to a volatile urban-slum-dwelling population. This trend greatly exacerbated an already latent set of political instability conditions.[7]

Even before the economic performance difficulties of 1977, the political economy framework would have classified Iran as being in minor disequilibrium because of the country's high potential for political instability. Such internal shock projections or forecasts are based primarily on an analysis of the sociopolitical context. The nine variables within the sociopolitical context are strongly supported by qualitative and/or statistical theory as being significantly related to mass political violence.[8] On a comparative basis, one would have had to rate Iran as high on eight of the nine variables, that is, except for the role of the military, the sociopolitical context had a very high potential for instability, as Table 13 shows.

In the table, Mexico, a country which subsequently became a major player in the international debt crisis, is compared to Iran. Mexico had a much lower instability potential than Iran for a number of reasons. Mexico is not socially diverse; there are no large ethnic-tribal groups facing strong discrimination. The ruling elite through the PRI has considerable legitimacy as the offspring of the Mexican revolution. Massive and overt elite repression is also low, and no major domestic disturbance had occurred in the recent past (within a generation). Opposition discontent is largely channeled and co-opted through the political, electoral system. In Iran, on the other hand, all of these factors (social diversity, congruent cleavages, elite legitimacy, elite repression, past internal war, and political system) were strong potential causes of instability.

By early 1980, moreover, Mexico was apparently on the way to achieving the country's primary strategic objectives of economic-political independence

Table 13
Comparative Political Instability Potential

Variable*	Iran-1977	Mexico-1984	Argentina-1984	Turkey-1985	South Korea-1985
Social diversity	High	Low	Moderate	Moderate	Low
Congruent cleavages	High	Low	Low	High	Low
Income distribution	High	Moderate	Moderate	Moderate	Moderate
Political system	High	Low	High	Moderate	Moderate
Past internal war	High	Low	Moderate	Low	Moderate
Elite repression	High	Low	Low	High	High
Elite illegitimacy	High	Low	Low	High	High
Role of military	Low	Low	High	Moderate	Moderate
Role of land reform	High	Moderate	Low	Moderate	Low
Over-all rating	High	Low	Moderate	Moderate	Moderate

*See Appendix A for a glossary of these terms.

and modernization through debt financing and import substitution. Of course, this prospect had been made possible largely by the recent discovery of vast petroleum reserves in a world environment of rapidly escalating oil prices. In short, because of a change in the physical and international context, a political and economic situation that had been fairly dismal in 1976–77 was turned around. Indeed, the only way a strategy such as that adopted by Mexico could succeed in the long term would be for a country to possess significant physical resources. Given Mexico's development plans and projects for the 1980s, the proven oil reserves were significant enough for the country's strategy to succeed, assuming oil prices remained near or above the 1980 level. A country risk analyst looking at Mexico in 1980 thus should have focused on the possibility of an external shock, with a dramatic fall in oil prices and markets being the most damaging and likely contingency. This would have been the correct focal point of analysis because the other key questions would have been resolved in a positive way. These questions were: Is economic performance meeting strategic goals? Are strategic goals and policies internally consistent? Does the strategy fit the context? What is the probability of adverse political change?

A major operational difficulty in this recommended approach is the correct identification of a country's or political elite's goals. A political system and ruling group that has been in power for a substantial period of time, however, usually has a track record of goal and policy pronouncements as well as actions that indicate the seriousness of those stated goals, all of which greatly facilitates the identification of the country's strategic mission. In assessing the Shah's goals, for example, one had a great deal of information over the years clearly pointing to a desire to achieve rapid economic growth and regional military supremacy in order to reach "big power" status within his or at least his son's lifetime.

On the other hand, political regimes that have only recently come to power are generally more difficult to assess. The Raul Alfonsín government in Argentina demonstrates this difficulty quite well. During the first year or so after Alfonsín became president, many Argentine experts analyzed his intentions and motives incorrectly. Instead of being either a political hack, ideologue, or opportunist, Alfonsín has proved to be a genuine and insightful nationalist sincerely dedicated to the economic and political development of his country. If Alfonsín was simply an ideologue or opportunist he would have approached the crucial decisions of 1984 far differently. These involved the economic and political tradeoff between the need to meet IMF targets and the political imperative of staying in power. A politically popular move, at least in the short term, would have been the repudiation of the IMF program and perhaps a moratorium on the external debt as well. Such a move, however, despite the fact that of all the major debtor countries Argentina would best survive a policy of economic autarchy, would have had very noticeable and adverse economic consequences. In shunning that tactic and in continuing to follow the September 1984 IMF agreement, Alfonsín faced far greater political risks than did President de la Madrid of Mexico, for example, when he complied with the November 1982 IMF agreement after becoming president in December. This fact is reflected in Table 13 regarding Mexico's and Argentina's relative potential for political instability. Alfonsín as ideologue or opportunist, therefore, was unlikely to present the Sourrouille Plan of January 1985, which led to the Austral reforms and the new IMF agreement of June 1985. By the spring of 1986, all external debt arrears were paid, and Argentina's economic and financial system had made significant strides toward more stable growth.

The correct identification of goals thus has great importance and poses problems when dealing with new regimes in particular. If the analyst remains highly uncertain about the strategic mission being sought in a country, that factor can become one of the critical drivers in a scenario-development exercise. In doing so assumptions and target events for different drivers or goal outcomes can be identified and planned for by the manager.

INTERNATIONAL LENDING DECISIONS: PAST AND PRESENT CASES

A major advantage of the conceptual framework and classification scheme just presented is the relatively easy application it has to international lending decisions. Although a bank's position on any particular loan will be strongly influenced by its management culture and overall portfolio, in general, long-term lending at market or concessionary rates should be given to countries that are either in equilibrium or possible disequilibrium. Long-term lending to countries with a political economy in minor disequilibrium should be limited and ideally at above-average rates or spreads. No voluntary long-term debt should be extended to countries in either major or traumatic disequilibrium unless one

Figure 6
Loan Spread–Country Risk Decision Matrix

	Equilibrium or Possible Disequilibrium	Minor Disequilibrium	Major or Traumatic Disequilibrium
High Spreads	Proactive, aggressive loan policy (maximize long-term lending)	Precautionary long-term lending	Very selective long-term lending (perhaps turnaround cases only)
Average or Low Spreads	Meet Customer And competitive Needs	Selective long-term lending (perhaps top quartile only)	No voluntary long-term lending

sees substantial signs of improvement. In most situations of this type, however, only short-term loans or trade financing should be contemplated. These guidelines are depicted in Figure 6.

If these general decision rules had been applied to the Iran and Mexico cases, what recommendations would have resulted? Since Iran in 1977 was in minor disequilibrium, long-term lending to the country should have been made cautiously. Iran's country exposure limit should have been placed at a relatively moderate to low level. Iran, in fact, would have been one of the more risky countries in minor disequilibrium because three of the five conditions for that classification were present: economic performance was not meeting strategic goals, political instability potential was high, and the strategy was adversely changing the context, making the political problem worse.

Mexico in 1980, on the other hand, was in either political-economic equilibrium or possible disequilibrium, depending on the oil price forecast. Mexico, therefore, would have been rated as an extremely attractive long-term lending opportunity. After the fall in oil prices, however, long-term lending to Mexico should have been curtailed, and country exposure limits lowered. Even short-term loans and trade financing should have been closely scrutinized by early 1982, given the fact that Mexico had possibly drifted by that time into major disequilibrium, due to the prolonged seriousness of the oil glut and the poor management of the resulting crisis by the Portillo government.

Arguably, then, the new framework of political economy could have provided some warning signals to international lenders with regard to these two countries. If a bank had followed the logic of this approach, lending to both Iran and Mexico certainly would have occurred but not to the extent pursued by most major banks during the 1970s and early 1980s. Future applications of the conceptual framework may prove to be equally helpful.

A more predictive, future-oriented application of the framework can be demonstrated through the two dramatically different examples of Turkey and South Korea. Both countries now receive voluntary long-term loans from commercial banks, but they are sociopolitically and economically quite distinct. Whereas Turkey is in a turnaround situation, South Korea is experiencing boom times.

Table 14
Turkey 1985: Minor Disequilibrium

A. External shock not likely
B. Strategy fits the context
C. Policies are somewhat inconsistent
D. Economic management basically sound but economic performance drops
E. Political instability potential is relatively moderate

Turkey is classified as a country in minor political-economic disequilibrium, as shown in Table 14. This state of country creditworthiness is best revealed by an analysis of economic performance, which deteriorated to some extent in 1984 due to larger fiscal budget deficits and higher inflation than expected. The causes of this adverse economic performance trend were macroeconomic, related to pre–November 1983 economic management mistakes and minor external shocks in early 1984. In mid–1982 Turgut Ozal, the architect of Turkey's 1980 austerity program, was forced to leave the government when he refused to implement military demands for a bank bailout and more expansionist monetary policy. Ozal's replacement largely followed the wishes of the military, and annual money supply growth rates started to approach the 50 percent level in 1983, nearly matching the 1979 and 1980 rates. This came after two consecutive years in the 30 percent range in 1981 and 1982. The inflationary consequences of this spurt started to be felt in 1984. Then Ozal, who was back in power after being elected prime minister in November 1983, may have aggravated the inflationary situation in the summer of 1984. Because of rising global interest rates in the first half of the year, Turkey's debt-service obligation rose as well, and 1984 was the first payment year after the 1979 and 1981–82 rescheduling agreements (a total of $2.4 billion was due). These higher-than-expected debt-service obligations were financed through greater government budget deficits. The absolute amount of the deficit increased nearly 400 percent in Turkish lira and by over 100 percent in U.S. dollars in 1984, reversing a trend in which the public sector balance as a percentage of GNP had declined every year in the 1980–83 period. Thus fiscal policies in particular were not fully consistent with other policies designed to further Turkey's export-oriented growth strategy.

On the positive side, a number of factors were working in Turkey's favor to restore the country's creditworthiness. Other than the area of fiscal policy, Ozal's economic management policies were very sound. Shortly after his election, a number of economic policy reforms were enacted, including a lifting of most import controls, the ending of foreign exchange and many capital controls, the daily adjustment of the Turkish lira, and the enactment of new foreign investment incentives. In this context even the surge in the fiscal deficit could be viewed

Table 15
South Korea 1985: Possible Disequilibrium

A. External shock possible, not likely
B. Strategy fits context
C. Policies are consistent
D. Economic management sound and economic performance meeting goals
E. Political instability potential is relatively moderate

as a necessary tradeoff in meeting a critical debt-servicing obligation. Servicing current debt payments, which Turkey was able to do in 1984–85, is certainly a prerequisite for restoring a country's creditworthiness. In the first half of 1984, in fact, new sources of private bank capital exceeded $1 billion, and this increase in foreign commercial debt largely financed the higher fiscal budget deficit, making its impact less inflationary.

The Turkish elite's country strategy also fits the context. An export-oriented, growth strategy is often essential for less developed countries funding their development through debt financing. In Turkey's case it is particularly essential because of the lack of great physical resources. The military's decision to give Ozal free rein to pursue his economic-liberalization goals has also been combined with a policy of selective democratization in the country. After the elections of 1983–84, internal security and foreign affairs are still in the firm hands of the military, and martial law conditions still hold in many Turkish provinces. Such a combination of participatory and repressive politics seems appropriate in a sociopolitical context of moderate instability potential. Lastly, a major external shock in terms of oil prices or war is certainly possible but not very likely in the next five years. Long-term lending to Turkey is now an acceptable proposition, particularly at expected rates of return that are higher than normal. Thus the biggest single loan to Turkey in 1984, which had a six-year maturity and was headed by Manufacturers Hanover for $300 million at an interest rate of 1.5 percent over *Libor*, was a wise one given the logic of this model. Turkey is in only minor disequilibrium, the trend line on balance is positive, and the loan was made at attractive rates.

South Korea presents another interesting application of the model. As Table 15 shows, South Korea's state of creditworthiness is in the relatively attractive category of "possible disequilibrium." A number of positive factors contributed to this classification. First, an external shock, such as a war with North Korea or massive trade protectionism in developed countries, is, of course, possible, but these and other potential threats (oil shock, severe global recession) are not likely. In addition the country's export-driven, growth strategy via debt and equity financing fits the South Korean context very well. The formulation and implementation of economic policies, moreover, have been very consistent and effective in meeting basic goals. The quality of South Korean economic management is best demonstrated by the speed and extent to which the country's economy was turned around after and during the second oil shock and severe global recession of 1980–82. After a drop of 3 percent in real GNP in 1980, real growth averaged 7.3 percent a year over the 1981–84 period. Economic performance is meeting most other goals as well. Inflation continues to drop from the 20 percent levels of 1980 and 1981; the Consumer Price Index (CPI) rate was 7.3 percent in 1982, 3.4 percent in 1983, and 3 percent in 1984. At the same time, the public sector deficit and the current account deficit as a percentage of Gross Domestic Product (GDP) have been consistently falling. Moreover, South Korea's debt burden remains at an acceptable level; in fact the long-term debt-service ratio remains below or at 20 percent. Thus, in virtually all economic performance and policy respects, South Korea is an extremely attractive lending market.

For some, the major concern about South Korea lies in the sociopolitical sphere. As Table 13 indicates, however, an inordinate fear of South Korean instability is not warranted. South Korea, at worst, has a relatively moderate potential for instability. In the context of the political economy model, therefore, South Korea is a very attractive lending market. From this analysis, the $600 million syndicated loan extended to South Korea in the fall of 1984 at very favorable interest rates to the borrower made a good deal of sense. The economic performance and management of the country is very sound, and the underlying sociopolitical situation is relatively safe.

CONCLUSION

Country risk analysis for international banking has gone through many stages of development. The first known formal country risk assessment and management system was established at Citibank in 1974–75 by Friedman. Many other major banks quickly followed. Initially, the structured qualitative methodology was the most popular approach, but this changed after the revolution in Iran, when political factors were upgraded in importance. Most bankers, however, did not know how to upgrade the importance of political factors in a way that was systematic and highly interrelated with economic variables. As a result, many bankers turned to checklist, weighting systems, which allowed the systematic integration of political and economic variables, at least superficially. Recently, however, checklist systems have also become suspect because of their general failure to predict the international debt crisis. Some banks, out of exasperation, have dropped almost all long-term country analysis and focus almost exclusively on short-term (less than a year) economic forecasts. Other and most major banks still see the significance and need for longer-term and more comprehensive country risk analysis but continue to analyze countries with systems and methodologies that have failed in the recent past. The development of new approaches to country risk analysis is thus important.

The conceptual framework of political economy is one possible contribution, with a number of fundamental strengths. First, the framework is based on sound theoretical relationships and variables. Second, these variables constitute a comprehensive list of those factors most likely to have an important impact on international lending prospects. Third, the approach has a strategic and structural focus, which should allow a bank to optimize its long-term position through portfolio management techniques. Fourth, the classification scheme is both simple and sophisticated, so that fifth, the conceptual framework and classification scheme is managerial and action oriented. Sixth, the proposed approach has a conservative lending bias, which fits the perceived needs of the international banking community in the late 1980s.

NOTES

1. Irving S. Friedman, *World Debt Dilemma: Managing Country Risk* (Philadelphia: Council for International Banking Studies, 1983), p. 214.

2. David Lomax, ''Sovereign Risk Analysis Now,'' *The Banker*, January 1983, p. 36.

3. The model of political economy derives its inspiration from a number of sources; the most major, in order of importance, are: Max Weber, *Economy and Society* (New York: Bedminster Press, 1966); Barrington Moore, *Social Origins of Dictatorship and Democracy: Lord and Peasant in the Making of the Modern World* (Boston: Beacon Press, 1966); Samuel Huntington, *Political Order in Changing Societies* (New Haven: Yale University Press, 1972); Douglas Hibbs, *Mass Political Violence: A Cross-National Causal Analysis* (New York: John Wiley and Sons, 1973); and Bruce R. Scott, John W. Rosenblum, and Audrey T. Sproat, *Case Studies in Political Economy: Japan 1854–1977* (Cambridge, MA: Division of Research, Harvard Business School, 1980), pp. 7–17.

4. J. Alexander Caldwell, ''Assessing Country Creditworthiness,'' *The Journal of Commercial Bank Lending*, July 1983, p. 9.

5. J. Alexander Caldwell and J. Antonio Vallamel, quoted in *Euromoney*, April 1979, p. 139.

6. Francis Mason, quoted in *Euromoney*, July 1980, p. 14.

7. See Charles R. Kennedy, Jr., ''Multinational Corporations and Political Risk in the Persian Gulf,'' *International Journal of Middle East Studies*, Fall 1984, pp. 397–99.

8. See Hibbs, *Mass Political Violence*, pp. 3–17, 135–36, 181.

4

International Investment and Risk Assessment

In the 1980–81 period several business-oriented periodicals and newspapers reported that U.S. multinational corporations devoted significantly more resources to political risk assessment since the Iranian revolution of 1978–79. One business periodical termed this development the ''post-Shah surge in political risk studies.'' This surge occurred because the ''Iran shock—and the failure of the U.S. government to foresee it—rocked complacent corporate policy'' toward the political-risk function.[1] Other reports noted that ''more companies are methodically assessing the political and economic risks of investing abroad. For that job, many of them are hiring political scientists and former Foreign Service Officers on a full-time basis.''[2] ''It remained for the revolution in Iran,'' according to another major business periodical, ''to drive home the lesson in global survival. Now even the most seasoned multinationals are looking for better means to assess—and manage—their political risks.''[3] However, in the wake of these journalistic observations there were few systematic, empirical attempts to measure or test the reported upsurge in political risk assessment, and the exact nature or form of any such increase remains unclear. This chapter, therefore, is intended to resolve these uncertainties by reporting the details of an extensive and recent study of current political risk management practices within large U.S. multinational corporations. Analysis of these practices may also reveal strengths and weaknesses of past approaches so as to guide efforts to improve political risk management.

RECENT POLITICAL RISK RESEARCH AND METHODOLOGY

The most recent and comprehensive study on political risk was based on structured interviews with sixty-one companies in 1983.[4] Ninety-four firms were initially contacted by mail. These targeted companies were chosen on the basis of several criteria, most notably 1982 sales of at least $1.5 billion. Within that group of very large (*Fortune* top 250) companies, the next criterion of selection was that over one-third of a firm's total sales were abroad, making the company a major multinational corporation, or that the firm was a competitor in a global industry, when firms with at least one-third of total sales abroad hold one-third or more of world market share.[5]

The sample of sixty-one firms actually interviewed differed only slightly from the ninety-four companies initially contacted. The sixty-one-firm sample had average annual sales of $12 billion, versus $11 billion for the entire ninety-four companies. The firms actually interviewed, moreover, had sales abroad that averaged 31 percent of total sales, and a mean of twenty-four countries in which each firm had foreign direct investment (FDI), compared 30 percent of total sales abroad and FDI in an average of twenty-one countries for the ninety-four-firm target.

Among companies interviewed, the industries represented were varied. The industrial-equipment industry accounted for the highest number of corporations in the sample (twelve), followed by petroleum (ten), aerospace defense (six), petrochemicals (five), food-beverage (five), diversified consumer products (five), computers (four), construction and agribusiness equipment (three), rubber-tire (three), metal extraction (three), pharmaceuticals (three), and automobiles (two). Aggregating these industries into natural resource-based companies (petroleum, metal extraction), intermediate goods producers (petrochemicals, computers, machinery, tire), or final goods producers (consumer, auto, food-beverage, aerospace), the sample was again well diversified, with thirteen, twenty-seven, and eighteen firms in each category respectively.

In the initial mailing, a cover letter plus a three-page questionnaire guideline was sent to the chairman of the board or the chief executive officer, unless a prior contact within the company was available. The cover letter explained the nature of the study and requested a personal interview based on the questionnaire guideline. As a result, interviews were conducted with ten firms in face-to-face sessions, and fifty-one interviews were conducted by telephone. Multiple interviews with the same respondent or with separate individuals in each company were common because of the need to close gaps in earlier interviews or because many firms placed responsibility for political risk analysis in more than one department or individual. In companies with multiple locations for political risk analysis, one found a remarkable consistency in the responses of different individuals. For example, when different respondents within a firm were asked to rank an issue on a ten-point scale, at no time did the responses vary by more than one point. One can argue, therefore, that the study measures predominate organizational perceptions and practices, with only slight individual variations within organizations. When responses did vary, an average was taken for the firm as a whole.

THE EXTENT AND FORM OF POLITICAL RISK INSTITUTIONALIZATION

The political-risk function has been institutionalized when a department or individual has been given formal responsibility for corporate-wide political risk assessment. Of the sixty-one companies interviewed, forty-five or nearly three-quarters of the total sample, had formally institutionalized the political risk function by 1983. Most of the companies with political risk institutionalization (twenty-five firms or 56 percent), moreover, had created the current area of focused responsibility after 1978, perhaps indicating some increase in the number of firms doing formal political risk analysis since the Iranian revolution. Such a conclusion gains support from comparison with research conducted under the sponsorship of the Conference Board in 1978.[6] The Conference Board study headed by Stephen Kobrin reported that 55 percent of a 193-firm sample had institutionalized the political risk function, versus this study's 74 percent. Such comparisons, however, need to be made with caution because of possible sample bias, particularly given the differences in the mean size of firms in the studies ($12 versus $2.6 billion). In any case there is little evidence to suggest a true post-Shah surge in political risk analysis. What appears to be closer to the truth is that there has been a fairly continual increase in the number of major U.S. corporations institutionalizing the political risk function since the early 1970s.

One could argue, given the 1983 sample, that there was no surge in the number of firms who institutionalized the political risk function since 1978. In particular, five of the twenty-five firms that had created the current focal point of responsibility for political risk since the Iran shock had simply shifted that responsibility to a department or individual at a higher corporate level. In two firms the initial centers of political risk responsibility were kept but were now secondary in importance to a newly created position—which in both firms was called the vice president for international affairs—who reported directly to either the president or chairman of the board. Another firm completely disbanded the international department and in the process moved the formal responsibility for political risk to the corporate planning department. In two other corporations the international departments were not disbanded nor was their responsibility for political risk assessment totally removed, but after 1978 the primary focus for such assessment was located in corporate planning. Thus, depending on how one counts, there has or has not been a slight quantitative increase in the institutionalization of political risk since 1978. If one counts firms who institutionalized political risk for the first time together with firms who simply moved the focal point of such responsibility since 1978, then there has been a small increase; there has not been an increase if one does not count those shifts in focal responsibility.

If the Iranian revolution did not necessarily have a quantitative impact on the attention U.S. multinationals gave to political risk, there are indications that a significant qualitative change took place in the way firms approached its management. One such indication is the recent tendency to have only one center of political risk assessment, especially among corporations which have institutionalized the function for the first time since 1978. In fact all twenty firms studied that had most recently formalized political risk focused that responsibility in only one area or department. Conversely, of the twenty-five companies with an institutionalized political risk function before 1978, eight firms (32 percent) had

Table 16
Types of Political Risk Analysts (percent of total analysts)

TYPE	Pre-Iran	Post Iran
Part-time responsibilities only	89	46
Full-time political Intelligence unit	4	15
Full-time political risk coordinator	7	39

multiple locations. One corporation had as many as four locations; another had three. One wonders how serious, coordinated, and effective the management of political risk could have been in such situations. One would, therefore, expect under such circumstances a tendency for political risk to be only a part-time duty approached fairly haphazardly.

A further and related sign that major U.S. corporations are placing more emphasis on political risk assessment is revealed by comparing job and time responsibilities of designated political risk analysts in the periods before and after the Iranian revolution, as depicted in Table 16. Before 1979 nearly nine out of ten analysts looked at political risk as only a part-time duty; their political risk responsibilities were merely added to their primary duties. This compares to less than half of political risk assignments being part-time work in the post–1978 period. In short, it is more likely that firms who institutionalized political risk after the Iranian revolution made that responsibility a full-time job.

Such full-time political risk analysts can be of the coordinator or intelligence unit type. Political risk coordinators collect and synthesize data supplied by outside contacts, consultants, and line management. Intelligence units contain a number of specialists, including consultants, who generate original risk forecasts almost, if not entirely, independent of line management. Most firms, however, that designate someone to have full-time responsibility for political risk do not proceed by attempting to create such mini-CIA departments. Only 15 percent of assignments since the Iran shock were given to intelligence units; nearly two out of every five assignments since 1978 were designated as political-risk coordinators.

A prime example of a political-risk-coordinator approach was the system used at Dow Chemical.[7] The Dow approach, called the Economic, Social, and Political (ESP) Risk Assessment Program, was headed by the manager of the international business environment. This corporate-wide position was created in 1980, although the ESP approach had been used in the Latin American region since

1971. The manager of the international business environment was essentially a political risk coordinator who organized periodic country reviews and constantly monitored the international scene for the company on a full-time basis. The ESP system operated on four basic principles: a team approach was always used; teams were composed of Dow employees only, both from inside and outside the country in question; the country review followed a structured approach; and the final report was more qualitative than quantitative.

The political risk coordinator essentially initiated a country review by forming a team of between six and eight Dow employees. The composition of a particular team typically included the local country manager and two or three of his key people, plus ''outsiders'' from regional and corporate headquarters. The team was headed by the corporate political risk coordinator. After about a week-long brainstorming session in the country being reviewed, the team disbanded, and a country risk report was written under the primary responsibility of the political risk coordinator.

By contrast, a corporate political-intelligence unit attempted to generate its own risk forecasts, involving line managers in the process only marginally, if at all. A good illustration of such an approach, the Primary Risk Investment Screening Matrix (PRISM), was developed at American Can in 1978.[8] PRISM was basically a mathematical, computer model that screened about seventy countries in terms of American Can's particular interests. Quantitative scores fed into the computer were in part judgments collected from many different sources, including political risk services like BERI, BI, and WPRF. Essentially, PRISM then reduced around two-hundred variables into two indices: an index of ''economic desirability'' and an index of ''risk payback.'' Of the seventy countries monitored, American Can considered an investment in only the dozen countries that received the best PRISM ratings.

A slightly different and perhaps more sophisticated approach to forming a political intelligence unit was found at Shell Oil Company. The Shell approach was known as the ASPRO-SPAIR System, which involved the specification of an explicit model of project-specific political risk.[9] Shell identified nine events that could increase the probability of political risk to a particular oil project. These events included civil unrest losses, sudden expropriation, tax restrictions, controls on remittances, and oil trade restrictions. Model specification was achieved by developing a complete set of factors for each event—factors which, if they occurred, would raise the probability of the event happening. Each factor was then represented in the form of a dichotomy between two statements that either support or reject the event in question.

A panel, whose members were chosen on the basis of country expertise from a variety of backgrounds and professions, was then formed. Each panelist was asked to review independently each factor for each event and make judgments as to the likelihood of the event. A confidence score was given as well. These judgments were used to generate a density function for the event's probability along each factor. The density functions were then combined across factors using

Bayes Theorem to derive an estimate for each expert on all nine events and across experts to gain a panel-wide prediction. As at American Can, there was virtually "no use of line/operating management for political risk information."[10]

This facet of political risk management, more than any other, separates the intelligence-unit approach from political-risk-coordinator systems. At Dow Chemical and many other companies, line managers were an integral part of the political risk process. For political-intelligence units, they were not part of the process at all. Dow's ESP system, however, was unique. A more common approach to political risk coordination is represented by General Motors, where corporate staff, with a full-time political risk coordinator attached to the International Economic Policy Group, surveyed line management through a questionnaire format—shown in Appendix B.[11] The questionnaire was extremely long and detailed. In many cases the questions were based on political theory. Other questions were specific to problems faced by automobile companies. The questionnaire was very future- or forecast-oriented as well. Of the forty-five questions in "Part One: Assessment of Factors," thirty-two, or 71 percent, asked line management to make predictions about future developments. Moreover, "Part Two: Policy Issues" and "Part Three: Policy Environment" were quite sophisticated and structured, which in some respects followed the Prince Model developed by Coplin and O'Leary.[12] Although information thus collected from the line did not dominate the decision-making environment, it did have a major influence on final political risk ratings. The corporate staff also had many internal resources, outside contacts, and consultants to use in conjunction with line management perspectives when making political risk recommendations.

Although he was clearly a political risk coordinator as well, the formal head of political risk management at Xerox, the director of international relations, contrasted the GM approach strongly with that of his company. According to him there were five approaches to political risk management, called Models R, K, S, B, and C.[13] Model R was a reactive approach without any formal structure; it was considered the most common approach. Model K, named after Henry Kissinger, referred to a corporation's primary dependence on international advisory boards for political risk assessment. United Technologies Corporation was a good example of that approach. Model S, for Sherpa, was akin to a political-intelligence unit, whereas Model C was analogous to what has been called a political risk coordinator at Dow and GM. The Xerox coordinator, however, considered himself a practitioner of Model B, for "bottoms up." In Model B, the corporation was quite dependent on line management for political risk information. Of course, the director of international relations had to institutionalize and coordinate the reporting system that gauged line management's views. At Xerox, this system was called the Issues Monitoring System (IMS). As part of IMS, line managers not only reported political risk information but were involved in a series of negotiations with regional and corporate personnel over specific political risk objectives for each country. Significantly, the promotion, evaluation, and bonus/incentive system was in part tied to these objectives.

Although the specific way in which firms institutionalize political risk has varied considerably, the general pattern since 1978 of hiring more full-time analysts seems clear. This pattern, along with the tendency for firms to centralize political risk institutionalization since 1978, strongly suggests significant change in the way U.S. firms approach political risk management. It should also be stressed that there is no single correct approach to political risk management. For Xerox, using the so-called Model B approach made sense for a company with so many fifty-fifty joint ventures abroad; a strong bottoms-up approach accommodated the strong interests and views of local partners. For United Technologies, on the other hand, the Model K system seemed appropriate for a broad-based conglomerate, where recently acquired and fairly independent businesses would have resisted too strong a corporate role in this area. For companies like General Motors and Dow, however, the Model C approach is more conducive to corporate structures which have mostly wholly owned or majority-controlled subsidiaries.

EXPLAINING POLITICAL RISK INSTITUTIONALIZATION

Past research pointed to five variables which help explain why companies institutionalize the political risk function. As the Conference Board study reported,

> Inferences can be drawn about the characteristics of firms that have institutionalized the assessment functions. First, as one would suspect, they are likely to be larger and more international than those who have not. There is a significant relationship [at the .05 level] between the existence of an assessment group[s] and firm size [sales], the percent of sales generated abroad, and the number of countries in which the firm has operations.[14]

The 1983 research, however, did not find these variables to be helpful in explaining political risk institutionalization. In terms of firm size, as one can see in Table 17, no significant relationship was found. Of course, because of possible sample bias, this does not necessarily mean that earlier findings were wrong or no longer valid. In effect, the 1983 study may have only analyzed firms that lie above some threshold level of total sales that makes all companies equally likely to institutionalize political risk analysis.

The more international companies, defined in terms of the percent of sales generated abroad or the number of countries in which there is FDI, were also not more likely to institutionalize political risk relative to less internationally oriented firms, as Tables 18 and 19 reveal. Once again, however, these results do not necessarily refute earlier findings. The 1983 sample clearly contains more international firms than the Conference Board sample. For example, 58 percent of the firms in the Conference Board study had international sales that were less than a quarter of their total, versus only 31 percent of firms in the 1983 sample.

Table 17
Chi-Square Test, Total Sales and Environmental Risk Institutionalization

	or	% Inst.	
Smaller Firms	23	65	X^2 = .7
Medium Firms	29	79	(P = .80)
Large Firms	9	78	N = 61

Table 18
Chi-Square Test, Foreign Sales and Environmental Risk Institutionalization

	n	% Inst.	
Small Foreign Sales (under 25%)	19	84	X^2 = 1.88
Medium Foreign Sales (25-35%)	20	65	(P = .50
Large Foreign Sales (over 35%)	22	73	N = 61

Table 19
Chi-Square Test, Companies' FDI Countries and Environmental Risk Institutionalization

Companies with:	n	% Inst.	
Fewest FDI Countries (under 15)	22	68	X^2 = .45
Medium FDI Countries (15-30)	22	77	(P = .80)
Most FDI Countries (over 30)	17	76	N = 61

Table 20
Chi-Square Test, Industry Type and Environmental Risk Institutionalization

	n	% Inst.	
Natural Resources-Based (petroleum, metal-extraction)	13	77	X^2 = .01
Intermediate Goods Producers (chemical, computer, machinery, tire)	27	74	(P = .99)
Final Goods Producers (consumer, auto, food-beverage, aerospace)	18	72	N = 58

Table 21
Chi-Square Test, International Organization and Environmental Risk Institutionalization

	n	% Inst.	
Pre-International	12	83	
International Division I	4	75	X^2 = 2.78
International Division II	11	55	(P = .50
Global	34	77	N = 61

Kobrin also identified other possible explanations for political risk institutionalization, namely industry type ($X^2 = .10$) and the nature of the international organization ($X^2 = .001$).[15] As with the other variables, the 1983 research casts some doubt on these earlier findings, as reflected in Tables 20 and 21.

Putting possible sample bias aside, an alternative explanation exists for the differences in findings; it is that the institutionalization of political risk has become so widespread that past differentiating variables no longer hold. In other words as the political risk function became increasingly institutionalized during the post–1978 period, smaller and less internationally oriented firms caught up to the larger, more international corporations who institutionalized the function first. The 1983 data mildly support this contention. Firms that institutionalized political risk before the Iranian revolution had total sales averaging $14.5 billion, mean international sales of 30.95 percent, and FDI in an average of twenty-seven countries, versus total sales of $11.5 billion, international sales of 28.96 percent, and FDI in twenty-one countries for companies institutionalizing the risk function after the Iran shock.

Table 22
Chi-Square Test, SBU Approach and Environmental Risk Institutionalization

	n	% Inst.	
SBU	49	78	$X^2 = 4.19$
No SBU	12	58	(P = .05
			N = 61

Thus the 1983 study may suggest that external conditions or the demographics of the firm are not the current driving force behind the institutionalization of political risk. It is possible that instead of external factors, the internal dynamic within the firm, specifically within the planning process, is a better explanation of political risk institutionalization. In particular, as Table 22 shows, firms that approach strategic planning in terms of a portfolio of strategic business units (SBUs) are more likely to institutionalize the political risk function. As to why a portfolio or SBU orientation toward planning seems significantly related to political risk institutionalization, an explanation may be rooted in the very logic of the portfolio approach. When one explicitly divides businesses strategically in terms of separate and identifiable products, competitors, and markets, one is inclined toward formal political risk analysis. For example, several firms have defined SBUs to correspond to a large foreign subsidiary, given that it has a separate and identifiable product, market, and set of competitors. Formal political and country risk analysis naturally complements or follows such a strategic organizational design and mind-set. Actually, such a relationship between SBU-based planning and political risk institutionalization should not come as a surprise. Several scholars who have advocated a portfolio approach to planning have pointed out the need and greater capacity of an SBU-based system to deal with political risk issues.[16] Perhaps these rather conceptual, academic points are now being implemented by large U.S. multinationals.

STRATEGIC PLANNING AND POLITICAL RISK INTEGRATION

Besides a probable link between the rise of portfolio planning and the institutionalization of political risk, other interrelationships exist between strategic planning and the increasingly important political risk function. Strategic planning has been by far the most prevalent location for the institutionalization of political risk assessment, as Table 23 demonstrates.

The institutional focal point of political risk analysis, moreover, varied consistently across broad industry categories. Of firms that are natural resource based, intermediate goods, or final goods producers, 80, 70, and 61 percent

Table 23
Current Locations of Environmental Risk Analysis by Firm

Area	Number of firms	Percentage of 45 total
Planning	32	71.5
International Division, Department or staff	13	28.9
Finance-Economics	6	13.0
Government, External or Legal Affairs	9	20.0
Other	4	9.0

respectively focused the political risk function in planning. The location other than planning revealed certain patterns across industries as well. For example, five of the six intermediate goods producers who had not institutionalized political risk in planning had instead housed the function in governmental, external, or legal affairs. For final goods producers, four of five firms without a location in planning have centered political risk assessment in finance-economics departments.

An explanation for these variations across industries is most likely rooted in the industries' relative capital intensity, length of payback for investments, and degree of political sensitivity to host governments. For all three measures, there is a rather consistent decrease as one moves from natural-resource-based industries to intermediate, and then to final goods producers. Since final goods producers have relatively low capital intensity, short payback periods, and little strategic importance to countries, they can afford to be more financially driven in their management of political risk. Intermediate goods producers, on the other hand, tend to face critical bargaining situations with host governments because of their significant captive investments and political sensitivity A government-external, or legal-affairs location for such companies thus makes a good deal of sense. The even longer lead times, higher capital intensity, and greater strategic importance of natural-resource-based companies also would explain their emphasis on a planning location for political risk management.

The argument that there has been a qualitative change in the way political risk is managed is reinforced by the linkage between a portfolio-planning approach, political risk institutionalization, and a planning location for the political risk function. Of firms in the 1983 study that located political risk in planning, 94 percent used SBUs when making strategic decisions. Conversely, only 62 percent of companies that have institutionalized political risk somewhere other than in planning have adopted a portfolio approach. Since over half the firms have started SBU-based analysis in the 1978–83 period, there is a strong possibility that the development of portfolio planning is moving hand-in-hand with the rise not only in political risk institutionalization but also in its location in planning.

Table 24
Location Shifts in Environmental Risk Analysis by Firm

Area	Pre-Iran (%)		Post-Iran (%)	
Planning	15	(44.1)	17	(57)
International Division, Department or staff	6	(17.5)	7	(24)
Finance-economics	2	(5.9)	4	(13)
Government, External or Legal Affairs	8	(23.5)	1	(3)
Other	3	(9.0)	1	(3)
Total	34	(100)	30	(100)

Such a development seems directly linked as well to an increase in those analysts described as political risk coordinators, as opposed to intelligence units. For example, 83 percent of political risk coordinators were part of the planning function, whereas the reverse was true for intelligence units—80 percent of these units were located outside of planning. Obviously, many firms and their managers have found SBU concepts to be useful tools of analysis, but this is especially true for the political risk coordinator, who can use the SBU approach to integrate political risk assessments into firm and industry characteristics on a comparative basis. In other words political risk analysis is an intrinsic part of the SBU conceptual framework and thus a necessary function for many U.S. multinationals today.

A locational shift into planning is also reflected by the data. When one compares the locations for political risk analysis in firms that had formalized the function before and after the Iranian revolution, then one observes a slight increase in planning as the most preferred site, as shown in Table 24.

An increased preference for housing political risk analysis in strategic planning is further suggested by comparing the 1983 study with the research sponsored by the Conference Board in 1978. The Conference Board study found that the most popular locations for political risk assessment were international divisions or finance-economics departments, followed closely by planning. In the 1983 sample, however, a location in strategic planning is two and one-half and five and one-half times more prevalent than an international division or finance-economics location, respectively.

Whether firms house the political risk function in corporate planning, or in other departments, there are striking similarities in how they rate the importance of political risk to strategic decisions. Firms with a non-planning location for political risk rated that function a 6.9 on a ten-point scale, where ten represented an overriding factor that largely determined final strategic decisions and a one represented a factor not even considered. The mean rating for firms with political risk housed in planning was 6.7, meaning that planners take political risk very seriously whether or not the function is located in the planning department.

It should be noted that the importance of political risk for planning transcends not only the way firms locate the function in different departments but varies little across broad industry categories as well. Whereas the entire sample yielded a 6.8 mean rating, the mean ratings by natural resource-based firms, intermediate goods producers, and final goods producers were 6.95, 6.5, and 6.9 respectively. The view that the political risk function was a major ingredient in corporate strategy was nearly universal.

Given the importance of political risk to strategic planning, how does the integration of political risk into planning take place? Generally, companies were asked if political risk forecasts were integrated into planning by financial or nonfinancial means. Financial integration was operationalized as using political risk assessments to justify an adjustment in the discount rate or hurdle rate, or to require the buying of political risk insurance. Nonfinancial integration, on the other hand, included go/no-go decisions, equity participation decisions, joint venture partner selection, non-equity participation (license or management-service contract options), and coalition-alliance building. The majority of firms, thirty-one companies (51 percent), stressed nonfinancial integration, whereas nineteen companies (31 percent) emphasized financial adjustments. In addition three firms (5 percent) stated that only nonfinancial integration took place. No firm indicated a sole reliance on financial moves. Eight firms (13 percent), however, found both types of integration equally important. Given the increased tendency to locate political risk in strategic planning, the relative stress on nonfinancial integration is not surprising.

Even though the entire sixty-one-firm sample emphasized nonfinancial integration, this aggregation masks some interesting differences across industries. In particular financial integration was overwhelmingly more common among consumer product and food-beverage companies (80 percent of firms in both industries). In all other industries nonfinancial integration was just as likely or much more likely than financial adjustments. This pattern reflects the degree to which consumer product and food-beverage companies are financially driven. As was observed earlier, such companies, which comprise the majority of final goods producers, are unlike most other industries in that their foreign investment or exposure level is relatively small given low capital intensity. As a result, their investment payback is achieved in a relatively short period of time. These consumer-based industries, moreover, are not typically strategic or politically sensitive to the host government. They are thus better able to stress financial integration compared to large, more capital-intensive investment industries, which are more likely to make nonfinancial moves to protect their longer-term, fixed-asset position.

MANAGERIAL PERCEPTIONS OF POLITICAL RISK

The type of political risk event that managers perceive to be most important to their company is related to firm characteristics and industry conditions in a pattern that mirrors the trend just discussed. Namely, the more politically sensitive, vulnerable industries are the most likely to rate variables associated with macro, extra-legal risk (political stability and FDI attitudes) as being highly important. In these cases, political risk forecasts are typically integrated into strategic decision making through nonfinancial means, such as entering into a joint venture to reduce the firm's exposure or visibility.

Only two industries rated political stability or FDI attitudes as being clearly the most important political risk considerations, as shown in Table 25. All other industries indicated that the more legal, governmental kinds of risks had the greatest impact on their firms, except tire and aerospace defense companies, which rated political stability as equal with foreign exchange, labor, and trade policies. In fact profit/exchange controls were given in most industries (petrochemical, industrial equipment, autos, food-beverage, and consumer products) as being the most significant risk event. Overall, however, political stability and profit/exchange controls were virtually identical in importance when computing the mean score for the entire sample.

These aggregate results exhibit both similarities and differences with the Conference Board study. As the Conference Board reported, the three most important risk events are political stability, FDI attitudes, and profit/exchange controls.[17] A big difference, however, lies in the relative weighting of these three concerns. Whereas the Conference Board showed political stability and FDI attitudes as equally the most significant event, the 1983 study finds political stability and profit/exchange controls as the top-rated risks. A stark difference in the two studies centers on the relative importance of administrative procedures, which includes the arbitrariness of regulations, the degree of bureaucratic red tape, and the extent of corruption. In the Conference Board study these concerns were rated the lowest of all those variables listed in Table 25. In 1983, however, administrative procedures are rated as just as important as tax policy, whereas in the earlier study, tax policy was three times more important than these various types of bureaucratic obstacles.

There are two possible explanations for these differences. First, managerial perceptions have changed because of subsequent events and laws, such as the international debt crisis and the Foreign Corrupt Practices Act. Second, the increased significance attached to both profit/exchange controls and administrative procedures may underlie a general view that legal-governmental risk is becoming a more threatening aspect of the external environment.

There were also a number of interesting idiosyncrasies in several industries. While petroleum companies rated political stability as the most crucial risk factor, tax policy was a fairly close second (3.0 versus 2.7). Perhaps the relatively high rating for tax policy reflects the oil industry's long-term sensitivity to and experience with such issues. The computer industry, on the other hand, was unusual in that it rated trade policy as being clearly the most important variable (3.0). This emphasis on trade is perhaps explained by the industry's strong integrated sourcing strategy. Certainly, the high importance of trade to the aerospace-defense industry (2.5) must be related to their large, centrally sourced export

Table 25
Managerial Perceptions of Risks Across Types of Industry

Type	Petroleum	Petro-chemical	Construction Agriculturial Equipment	Industrial Equipment	Food Beverage	Consumer	Pharma-ceutical	Autos	Aerospace Defense	Metals	Computer	Tire	Total
Political Stability	2.9	2.2	2.0	2.6	2.2	2.6	3.0	1.5	2.5	3.0	2.8	2.0	2.53
FDI Attitudes	2.0	2.4	1.3	2.5	2.0	2.4	3.0	2.5	2.0	3.0	2.5	1.7	2.26
Profit/ Exchange Controls	2.1	2.8	2.0	2.9	2.8	3.0	2.0	3.0	2.3	2.3	2.5	2.0	2.52
Labor Policy	1.2	1.2	2.3	1.7	1.6	2.0	1.3	2.0	2.5	2.3	2.3	1.3	1.74
Tax Policy	2.7	2.0	1.7	2.1	2.0	1.8	2.0	2.0	1.7	2.0	2.3	1.7	2.08
Trade Policy	1.4	1.6	2.3	2.3	2.0	2.6	1.7	3.0	2.5	2.3	3.0	1.7	2.13
Administrative Procedures	2.2	1.8	1.7	2.1	1.6	2.0	2.0	1.5	2.2	1.3	2.0	1.7	2.08

activity. Not surprisingly, the agricultural equipment industry showed the same high concern for trade (2.3), undoubtedly due to similar motivations. Likewise, both aerospace-defense and agricultural equipment industries rated labor policy very high (2.5 and 2.3 respectively) because of common and unpleasant experiences with labor disputes in the U.S. and Europe. Lastly, the automobile industry was quite sensitive to trade issues as well (3.0) due to their accelerated integrated sourcing approach and their recent resort to government trade protection in the face of foreign competition. Managerial perceptions of political risk are strongly influenced by industry characteristics and firm experiences that follow a fairly logical, predictable pattern.

SOURCES OF POLITICAL RISK INFORMATION

Past research has indicated that corporate political risk analysts are highly dependent upon line/operational managers for providing information about political risks. The 1983 study confirmed that that essential relationship still holds. When companies were asked to rank their dependency on line/operational managers for political risk information on a ten-point scale, with one being no information from the line and ten being total dependence, the mean response was 5.48. Although that makes the line the single most important source of political risk information, the ranking also suggests a virtual balance between information supplied by line managers and by other sources, such as corporate staff, consultants, or other external sources of information from business, academia, and government.

The degree to which a firm is dependent on the line for political risk information is related to the political risk management system in place at the corporate level. For example, firms are most dependent on the line when there has been no institutionalization of the political risk function; their mean score was 7.1, versus 5.6 for companies with part-time analysts, 4.2 for firms with full-time coordinators, and 3.2 for corporations with intelligence units. Such a trend suggests that as corporate political risk capabilities increase, the dependency on the line diminishes. This is not to suggest that increasing corporate capabilities to the extent of forming an intelligence unit is an optimal development. Although intelligence units typically justify their relative lack of interaction with line managers on grounds of the line's tendency to be biased toward local projects or to be generally ill-equipped to do good political risk analysis, a low level of involvement by country and overseas managers in the political risk process exposes the firm to a number of possible problems. The corporate level may be missing an extremely important source of information, in that line managers readily understand the specific nature of the firm and the direct impact of political risk on the company. By contrast, country experts or consultants may know the specifics of the political environment very well but typically do not instinctively understand how to relate these risk assessments to the particular situation faced by the company or project. Perhaps more importantly, line managers should feel

Table 26
Chi-Square Test, SBU Approach and Political Risk Reporting

	N	%SBU	
Ad Hoc/Operational Reports	32	63	
			$X^2 = 5.47$
			P =(.02)
Strategic Reviews/Political Reports	22	91	

involved and influential in decision making if the implementation of political risk strategies are to be fully effective. In this sense the presence of a corporate political-intelligence unit may be counterproductive if it entails a tendency to neglect or ignore input from line management.

Given the continued and intrinsic importance of line managers in the political risk assessment process, a research project to investigate how and why political risk information flows from the line to the corporate level was launched in the summer of 1985. Most of the original sixty-one firms in the 1983 study were contacted (some companies no longer existed due to mergers), and a fifty-four-firm sample was completed by November 1985.

Despite the relative dependence on line managers for political risk information, most firms (32 or 59 percent) collected data and assessments on political risk from overseas subsidiaries only on an ad hoc basis through routine, operational reports. On the other hand, seventeen firms (32 percent) required, either formally or informally, that political risk considerations be explicitly included in strategic reviews. In five companies (9 percent) the completion of separate political risk reports by the line was a formal requirement. Since political risk reports were made in conjunction with the strategic review process, this system is not substantially different from firms that only integrate political risk concerns within a planning document or report.

As to why some firms have a more formal and ongoing political risk reporting system than others, the explanation is tied to the way the corporate level is organized to conduct strategic planning and political risk analysis, as Tables 26, 27, and 28 reveal. There is a significant statistical relationship at the .02 level between a portfolio or SBU approach to planning and the political risk reporting system. In light of the earlier relationship established between SBU planning and political risk institutionalization, this result should come as no surprise. One would expect a portfolio-based planning system not only to encourage the development of formal political risk analysis at the corporate level but to lead to the requirement of systematic political risk reporting from the line as well. Likewise, the strong statistical relationship (at the .01 level) between political

Table 27
Chi-Square Test, Political Risk Institutionalization and Political Risk Reporting

	N	%PRT	
Ad Hoc/Operational Reports	32	59	
			X^2=9.94
			P = (.01)
Strategic Reviews/Political Reports	22	96	

Table 28
Chi-Square Test, Political Risk Institutionalization Within SBU/Planning Departments and Political Risk Reporting

	N	%SBU	
Ad Hoc/Operational Reports	32	31	X^2=11.04
			P =(.001)
Strategic Reviews/Political Reports	22	77	

risk institutionalization and the method of political risk reporting makes a good deal of sense. Surely, full-time political risk analysts at the corporate level will want top management to require formal political risk reports. Putting the two explanations together—that is, identifying the relationship between political risk reporting and political risk institutionalization within SBU-based planning systems—one found the greatest statistical significance of all (at the .001 level).

These findings become even more interesting when one realizes that no other factor or variable was even remotely related to a firm's approach to political risk reporting, as Tables 29 and 30 show. The more politically sensitive and vulnerable industries do not have formal, ongoing reporting systems to a greater extent than other industries. The political risk assessment methodology also fails as an explanation. When firms at the corporate level were asked to rate the degree to which their methodology is quantitative or qualitative, with a 10 being solely quantitative and a 1 being totally qualitative, the thirty-two companies with ad hoc operational reports had a mean score of 3.23 versus 3.98 for the twenty-two firms with political reports associated with the strategic review process. One might have hypothesized that more quantitatively oriented firms may have less need for formal political risk reports from the line. A firm's degree of international exposure does not seem related to political risk reporting. In fact

Table 29
Chi-Square Test, Industry Type and Political Risk Reporting

	N	%AD HOC/OPS	%STRATEGIC REVIEWS/REPORTS
Natural Resource-Based (Petroleum, Metal Extraction)	13	77	23
Intermediate Goods Producers (Chemical, Computer, Machinery, Tire)	22	59	41
			X^2=1.9 (P =.50)
Final Goods Producers (Consumer, Auto, Food-Beverage, Aerospace)	17	53	47

Table 30
Political Risk Reporting Relationships (mean scores)

	AD HOC/ OPERATIONAL REPORTS	STRATEGIC REVIEW POLITICAL REPORTS
Political-Economic Scanning, Analyzing Methodology	3.23	3.98
Dependence on Line Managers For Political Risk Information	5.64	5.16
Importance of Political Risk-Economic Forecasts to Strategic Plans	6.72	6.59
% of International Sales	32.5	30.9
# of FDI Countries	25.3	22.8

the more internationally oriented firms, in terms of mean scores, tend to have an ad hoc system. Lastly, the importance of political risk forecasts to strategic plans is in no way related to line management responsibilities in the political risk area. An interesting irony is that firms that rate themselves more dependent upon line managers for political risk information have informal, ad hoc requirements.

In essence the political risk function and how it affects the entire organization, from the corporate staff to the line management levels, seems conditioned and shaped by the planning culture within the firm. One visible measure of a planning culture is the existence of portfolio concepts or formal SBUs within the organization. Such an approach to planning seems clearly and strongly related not only to political risk institutionalization at the corporate level but to the formal integration of political risk assessments by line management into the strategic planning process as well. The managerial and decision-making implications of these relationships are explored in the next chapter.

NOTES

1. *Business Week*, December 1, 1980, p. 69.

2. Ronald Alsop, "More Firms Are Hiring Own Political Analysts to Limit Risks Abroad," *The Wall Street Journal*, March 30, 1981, p. 1.

3. Louis Kraar, "The Multinationals Get Smarter about Political Risks," *Fortune*, March 24, 1980, p. 86.

4. Charles R. Kennedy, Jr., "The External Environment-Strategic Planning Interface: U.S. Multinational Corporate Practices in the 1980s," *Journal of International Business Studies*, Fall 1984, pp. 99–108.

5. William H. Davidson, *Global Strategic Management*, (New York: John Wiley and Sons, 1982), pp. 6–7.

6. Stephen J. Kobrin, John Basek, Stephen Blank, and Joseph La Palombara, "The Assessment and Evaluation of Non-Economic Environments by American Firms: A Preliminary Report," *Journal of International Business Studies*, Spring-Summer 1980, pp. 32–47.

7. John S. Schwendiman, "Managing Environmental Risk: Cases and Lessons for Corporate Strategy," *International Political Risk Management: New Dimensions*, Fariborz Ghadar and Theodore Moran, eds. (Washington D.C.: Ghadar and Associates, 1984), pp. 108–20.

8. *Fortune*, March 24, 1980, p. 92.

9. For an excellent discussion of the ASPRO/SPAIR system, see Stephen J. Kobrin, "Political Assessment by International Firms: Models or Methodologies," *Journal of Policy Modeling*, 2, no. 3, 1981, pp. 251–70.

10. Personal interview with a high-level manager at American Can, April 1983.

11. Gordon Rayfield, "General Motors' Approach to Country Risk," *Assessing Country Risk*, Richard Ensor, ed. (London: Euromoney Publications, 1981), pp. 129–34.

12. William D. Coplin and Michael K. O'Leary, "The World Political Risk Forecasting Service," *Political Risks in International Business: New Directions for Research, Management and Public Policy*, Thomas L. Brewer, ed. (New York: Praeger Publishers, 1985), pp. 163–92.

13. Daniel Sharp, "Business Environment Assessment," *Managing International Political Risk: Strategies and Techniques*, Fariborz Ghadar, Stephen Kobrin, and Theodore Moran, eds. (Washington D.C.: Ghadar and Associates, 1983), pp. 7–31.

14. Kobrin, et al., "Assessment and Evaluation of Non-economic Environments," p. 35.

15. Stephen J. Kobrin, *Managing Political Risk Assessment: Strategic Response to Environmental Change* (Berkeley: University of California Press, 1982), pp. 77–191.

16. Yoram Wind and Susan Douglas, "International Portfolio Analysis and Strategy:

The Challenge of the 80s,'' *Journal of International Business Studies*, Fall 1981, pp. 69–73; Peter Lorange, *Implementation of Strategic Planning* (Englewood Cliffs, NJ: Prentice Hall, 1982), pp. 6, 62; William H. Davidson, *Global Strategic Management* (New York: John Wiley and Sons, 1982), p. 5; and Charles Hofer and Dan Schendel, *Strategic Formulation Analytical Concepts* (St. Paul: West Publishing Company, 1978), pp. 55–60.

17. Kobrin, et al., ''Assessment and Evaluation of Non-economic Environments,'' p. 41.

5

Political Risk Strategy

International banks and manufacturing firms face contrasting kinds of exposure and risk when operating abroad. Banks are exposed almost solely through loans made to foreign borrowers, both private and public, while manufacturing firms are more directly exposed in a myriad of ways—trade restrictions, physical dangers to employees, the compromising of proprietary technology, the destruction or expropriation of investment property, and so on. Chiefly because of the more or less unidimensional nature of bank exposure, country and political risk assessments have a relatively uniform impact on international lenders. An exception to this uniformity may involve differences between short-term and long-term lenders; however, the international debt crisis of the 1980s has shown that short-term lenders often face the same risks as long-term lenders, since reschedulings have on occasion lumped trade financing and term loans into one package.

Clearly, in contrast to the experience of banks, the impact of political risk assessments varies greatly among manufacturing firms. Each faces a highly individualized set of risks because of numerous factors, including industry structure or economics, project-specific characteristics, and management activity. In short manufacturing firms confront deeper, more complex issues than do banks when assessing political risk.

Banks and manufacturing firms also differ in another fundamental way with regard to assessing political risk. Manufacturing firms typically are working with a longer time horizon. Whereas natural resource, industrial production, and marketing companies are all often in a country to do business indefinitely, a bank lends only for a specified contract period. Banks, therefore, tend to focus a good deal of attention on short-term balance-of-payments analysis, while manufacturing firms may be more concerned with long-term societal trends and the public policy process.

Banks and manufacturing companies also face many common concerns about political risk. Most fundamentally, of course, the macroeconomic and political environment of the country in which the business relationship exists is vitally important to both kinds of firms. It is when analysis moves on to questions of the environment's impact on specific companies that crucial differences between banks and manufacturing firms emerge.

ASSESSING THE MACROINVESTMENT ENVIRONMENT

The first, most basic step in assessing the macroeconomic and sociopolitical environment of a country has been described in the conceptual framework of political economy and its associated classification scheme. These will provide an analyst with a comprehensive, comparative road map for judging country risk. However, they can also be the basis for an even more in-depth, sophisticated political analysis. A discussion and demonstration of this level of analysis seems appropriate, given the longer-term and more complex risks faced by industrial, nonfinancial firms, in contrast to banks.

In Chapter 3, nine major variables were listed within the sociopolitical context and were empirically and statistically related to political instability. Countries were then compared along each variable to reach overall ratings on their potential for political instability. No attempt was made, however, to aggregate these variables conceptually into a unified and interrelated package or framework. The concepts of political development and modernization may help forge such a theoretical synthesis.

Political development is here defined by a system's capacity to absorb and adapt to technological change, or modernization.[1] Advances in education and scientific applications of knowledge increase both the demands upon a political system, or participation, and the system's capacity to deal with those demands, or institutionalization. Political development can be described by the relationship between these factors, as shown in Figure 7.

The degree of institutionalization within all political systems can be defined by the coherence, autonomy, adaptability, and complexity of its organizations and procedures.[2] The more internally unified the organization or the less dissension that exists among its members, the more the organization is institutionalized. At the same time, organizational autonomy from other social groupings means more institutionalization and often leads to a more coherent organization as well, due to the greater esprit de corps and the shields against outside intrusions that tend to develop within autonomous organizations. Highly adaptable organizations, moreover, tend to survive environmental changes and thus are prone to more institutionalization. Highly institutionalized organizations exhibit characteristics of longevity, generational changes in leadership, and shifting functional responsibilities. Lastly, complex organizations are more institutionalized than simple ones because many different organizational subunits facilitate control over members and greater adaptability.

Strong institutions can either stimulate, adapt to, or suppress participation.

Figure 7
Model of Political Development

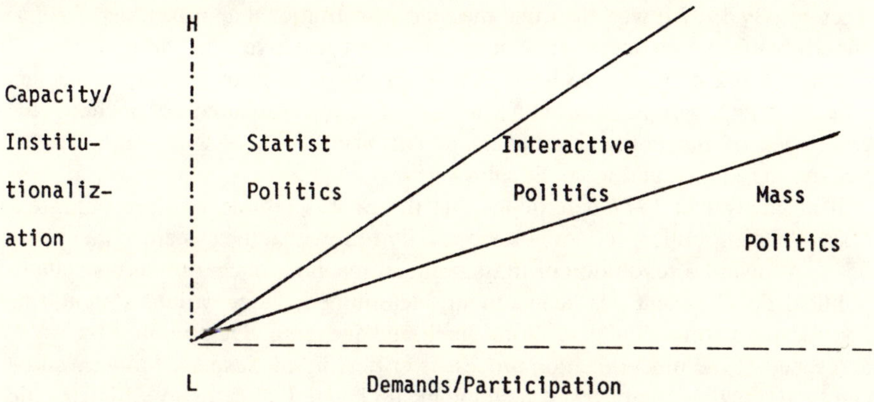

Political participation takes several forms (voting, petitioning, attending meetings, or demonstrating, etc.) but can be generally classified as demands on a system or system supports. One should note that a modern political system can be highly participatory without being liberal democratic. Mass mobilizational regimes can encourage or even mandate high levels of political participation. One should also stress that political participation in the form of demands will inevitably increase as societies modernize, a process typically associated with mass migrations to cities and higher educational and literary levels. Institutions, therefore, should be present to satisfy and adapt to participatory demands or to channel rising participation in a way that supports the system. Otherwise, the probability of political instability increases dramatically. Ideally, participation should be the means by which a political system builds stronger institutions.[3]

The most politically developed and stable societies, therefore, exhibit a dynamic balance and tension between participation and institutionalization, when the demands upon the system are roughly equal to the system's capacity to meet those demands. In such a situation political institutions and participation dialectically influence or shape each other. This situation can be called interactive politics. Statist politics, in which institutional capacity directs or controls participation, is more prone to instability. In some instances participation is repressed or stifled by the institutional and coercive capacity of the state, and a revolutionary or mass political reaction can result. Thus a society can jump from statist to mass politics, the third category of political development, in a short period of time. By implication, mass politics is potentially the most unstable system. If demands upon the system are excessive and uncontrolled, anarchy or revolution will occur. Charismatic and strong leadership is usually needed to steer a mass political system into constructive institution building.

The case of Iran amply illustrates the political development problems associated with imbalanced statist politics. During the 1970s the Shah's regime became more and more repressive and tried to force participation into a single party system. As the Shah's coercive measures intensified, so did the terrorist reaction. By 1977 it was clear that the Shah's institutional approach was failing, but a change in tactics at that point proved ineffective. As Amir Taheri, a journalist with close ties to the Shah, observed in 1977 and 1978, "The fact remains the government structure in Iran is still unprepared for meeting the exigencies of the political decade that lies ahead." In essence Iran was an "economic giant" and a "political dwarf."[4]

If an analyst in 1977 determines that the Shah's regime was practicing excessive statist politics, it does not necessarily follow that the system is inevitably heading toward a revolution or mass political reaction; once a society's state of political development has been roughly determined, other variables should be considered to give this state more depth and meaning. Determining the stage and speed of the modernization process is critical in this respect. Modernization can be defined as a process of technological change that leads to a higher ratio of inanimate to animate sources of power and to a greater multiplication of effort as an effect of tool application.[5]

Three stages of modernization can be generally distinguished: precommercialization, in which the agrarian sector is still characterized by predominant subsistance-barter relationships and the urban-industrial sector is very small or nonexistent; preindustrialization, in which market and cash transactions dominate agriculture but the urban-industrial sector is still smaller than the agricultural or primary sector; and postagricultural, in which the majority of national wealth or income and the labor force is found in the secondary-tertiary sectors of the economy. The most potentially unstable societies are found in the middle stage of modernization, when the epoch-making transition from an agrarian to an industrial state is taking place. All major revolutions (French, Russian, and Chinese, as well as Iranian) have occurred at this point in the modernization process.[6]

Looking at modernization and political development together, it is clear that the most unstable societies are those characterized by mass politics and in the preindustrial stage. Mass political systems in the precommercialized stage are virtually nonexistent, whereas mass politics in urban-industrial societies is usually confronted by an institutional repressive reaction, either in the form of a military coup or by government suspension of constitutional rights and liberties. Statist political systems in the preindustrial stage have a high potential for political instability as well, but the exact potential for instability depends on other variables which we will consider shortly. Statist, precommercial societies, on the other hand, are very common and typically quite stable until the drive to industrialization begins. Statist, industrial societies, moreover, are also relatively stable, as are most interactive political systems, regardless of the modernization stage. Table 31 depicts these comments as a matrix of political development and mod-

Table 31
State of Political Development, Modernization, and Degree of Political Instability Potential

	Statist	Interactive	Mass
Pre-Commercialization	Low	Low	High
Pre-Industrial	High	Moderate	High
Urban-Industrial	Moderate	Low	Moderate

Table 32
A Political Development-Modernization Classification of Selected Countries

	Statist	Interactive	Mass
Pre-commercialization	Japan, 17th-18th Century	Zula Kingdom, 19th Century	Japan, 16th Century
Pre-industrial	Iran, 1954-1977	India, 1948-1975	Iran, 1978-79
Urban-industrial	Spain, 1936-77	United States, 20th Century	Poland, 1978-79

ernization that yields high, moderate, or low potential for political instability and Table 32 gives some historical examples.

The rural tenure structure is an additional consideration that can be key in determining the probability that a society can make a nonrevolutionary transition from a predominantly agrarian to an urban-industrial state. Such a transition usually requires fundamental land reform, which is the transformation or fundamental shift in basic tenure, power, and wealth relationships among various agricultural groups and classes. In most countries land reform is essential because it is needed to meet the food and labor requirements of a more modernized society.

Three types of land-reform situations generally exist. First and the most stable is avoidance, or lack of land reform, when the agricultural sector is extremely small and other primary-sector means of generating wealth are available (e.g., oil). Such cases are relatively rare, with Saudi Arabia being one such example. The most unstable situation is one in which a political system has avoided land reform but contains a large traditional agrarian structure that is experiencing intense pressures of commercialization as the transition toward a predominantly urban-industrial society takes place. Such was the case in prerevolutionary France, Russia, and China. A more problematic situation of instability exists when agrarian commercialization is being consciously directed by the state within an overall land-reform package, as was the case in Iran. Other variables are needed to assess such a program's chances of success or the probability of reaching the postagricultural stage of modernization without violent revolutionary change.

An important additional consideration is the degree of social diversity in the country. Four different aspects of diversity should be studied: ethnic, regional, religious, and linguistic. Obviously, the more diverse a society is, the more difficult it is for the state's institutions to meet satisfactorily the population's participatory needs and demands.

The probability that a high degree of social diversity will cause a violent mass political reaction in a system of statist politics is heightened if two additional factors are present. First, recent violent upheavals or internal war make revolutionary change much more likely. In addition the number and intensity of congruent cleavages, when socioeconomic classes overlap with regional-ethnic-linguistic-religious groups, also greatly increase the likelihood of a mass political reaction. Determining the number of congruent cleavages is primarily a counting procedure, while their intensity is measured by the relative percentage of the population represented by status groups that are predominantly lower class. Although both factors, recent internal war and congruent cleavages, make political mobilization on the basis of social diversity more likely, the extent and intensity of congruent cleavages is subject to policy intervention. State-directed land reform is one important way the potential instability impact of such cleavages can be mitigated.

These variables or concepts can be illustrated within the Iranian context. The Shah in the 1970s was handicapped by the legacy of two previous incidents of mass upheaval or internal war. Both in 1952 and 1963 the Shah ordered his troops to machine gun demonstrators in the streets of Tehran. Such actions created a hard-core constituency in permanent opposition to the Shah and increased the probability of a mass political reaction. The presence of many important congruent cleavages had the same effect. Ethnic, tribal, and linguistic minorities, such as the Azarbaijanis, Kurds, Turkomans, Baloch, and Arabs, also had mean incomes much lower than the Persian population. Social differences were more antagonistic as they overlapped with economic class distinctions. Demands for greater socioeconomic equality and/or political autonomy were particularly intense from these groups, as was their general opposition to the Shah once their demands were not met.

Compounding the Shah's political development problem was the growing pattern of class inequity across the spectrum of Iranian society. Despite government claims to the contrary, nearly all independent observers pointed to the Shah's failure to adequately distribute the benefits of the oil boom to most Iranians. Rampant inflation undermined the real incomes of the middle class and industrial workers, while the number of urban slum-dwellers quickly mounted. Such trends provided fertile ground for the Shah's core opposition to exploit.

Another variable making the Shah's system more potentially unstable concerns the legitimacy of the state. Manifestations of the state's loss of legitimacy include large and rising incidents of antigovernmental activity, such as acts of terrorism, riots, general strikes, and demonstrations. In Iran several factions saw the Shah without having legitimate authority, a belief expressed by the rising number of terrorist incidents during the 1970s and by the growing religious demonstrations that started in January 1978.

The type of political system also influences the instability potential of statist politics. Political systems are grouped here into three types: authoritarian-traditional (Shah's Iran, Czarist Russia, Chiang Kai-shek's China, Louis XVI's France); authoritarian-mobilizational (Soviet Union, People's Republic of China, Cuba, Iraq); and liberal-democratic (United States, United Kingdom, Japan, India). Statist politics have a much lower probability of instability when the ruling elite governs an authoritarian mobilizational state, in which strong institutions direct and control massive participation in the system through one broad-based political party. The Shah was attempting to move Iran in this direction with the creation of the National Resurgence Party, but the effort failed to generate massive and supportive participation in the political system. The Shah simply lacked either the legitimacy or the strong ideological vehicle that could attract enough support for his regime.

A final factor to be considered in this model of political development is the role of the international environment. Besides macroeconomic interdependencies, this variable also measures the threat of war and subversion. Obviously, external forces can exacerbate basic internal causes or sources of instability such that the probability of social diversity and congruent cleavages leading to internal war and/or antigovernmental protests dramatically increases, as was the case in Russia and China. In Iran, on the other hand, foreign support of urban terrorist activity and religious dissent was present but was not a major factor in the Shah's downfall. The Iranian revolution was almost entirely an internally generated event, much like the French Revolution.

The model of political development is thus a useful analytical tool that helps synthesize the variables related to political risk and that essentially encapsulates the dynamic among a country's context, strategy, and performance. Political rulers, explicitly or not, choose how to deal with the unavoidable forces of modernization and participation. This choice may be the most crucial strategic decision a political system can make. In fact, to a large degree, the interrelationship between institutionalization, participation, and modernization will shape or define the limits of macroeconomic performance. A business manager analyzing the political risks of operating in a country needs to be at least aware of these choices and concepts.

ASSESSING MICROINVESTMENT RISK

Studying the general macroeconomic and sociopolitical environnment is only the first fundamental task a corporate political risk analyst must undertake. In particular countries do not have risks, nor in many respects do industries. Instead, companies and projects have risks. This observation is increasingly true as the frequency of massive, across-the-board nationalizations or expropriations by countries has dramatically decreased over the last decade. At the same time, adverse intervention by host governments against individual multinational corporations has not only increased in intensity, but has become a more widespread practice throughout the world. It appears that "the variation in intervention experiences *within* most countries is greater than the differences *between* national average levels of intervention. A nation's average level of intervention is a poor guide to what individual subsidiaries experience there."[7]

Moreover, the form of this intervention has been changing. Increasingly in the late 1970s and 1980s, countries turned away from expropriation as an intervention tactic and chose to rely instead on "localization" measures, such as equity ownership laws, local content rules, intercountry financial controls, and expatriate employment regulations. These laws, controls, and regulations are increasingly enforced within or preceded by a negotiation process; enforcement via unilateral government action is becoming less frequent, especially in the most attractive markets or countries with relatively advanced, sophisticated political institutions.

In this changing environment, many of the traditional approaches to political risk management used by multinational corporations have become less and less relevant. For example, two such approaches were avoidance and political risk insurance. Avoidance, or not investing in those countries considered the most likely mass expropriators, is not very useful when that intervention tactic is no longer prevalent. In fact avoidance can be counterproductive to a firm's interests when applied to the new sets of intervention risks, since the countries most likely to intervene against foreign business interests today are also the biggest, most attractive markets with the greatest profit and strategic opportunities.

Political risk insurance, an effective hedge against expropriation, is less effective in protecting the firm against the newer, more subtle forms of government intervention. Given their subtlety, these kinds of risks are more difficult to define and measure. As a result, disputes can arise between the insurer and the firm over claims, with the Dow experience in Chile during the early 1970s being one notorious example. Because of many of these difficulties, the cost of political risk insurance has risen substantially as well.[8]

Multinational corporations, therefore, need to develop approaches to political risk management that better address the increasing importance of legal-governmental, as opposed to extra-legal, risk. In many ways, a new era of multinational-host government relations has begun. In the 1950s and early 1960s, there was an era of multinational domination, followed by an era of confrontation in the late 1960s and early 1970s. Now one sees an era of negotiations. In fact the predominance of negotiations when countries enforce international business laws and regulations implies that these new forms of risk can be managed through a give-and-take, bargaining process. As a result, bargaining power analysis and concepts should form the centerpiece of any new approach to political risk management.

A bargaining power approach has long been recognized as an important focal point for analysis of multinational-host government relations.[9] Until recently, however, no empirical study of a large number of companies in different countries existed to validate or clarify this focus. Fortunately, two such studies published in 1982 reveal substantial support for the relevance of bargaining power theory when assessing government-business negotiations. Thomas Poynter's study of 104 firms in three African and one Asian country reached conclusions that were very similar to Nathan Fagre's and Louis Wells' analysis of 178 companies operating in Latin America.[10] Certain characteristics were found to increase corporate bargaining power in both studies. The first important factor associated with corporate bargaining power was operational and managerial complexity, which Poynter identified on a qualitative, case-by-case basis. Fagre and Wells, on the other hand, observed a similar relationship but quantified it, focusing their analysis on product differentiation, operationalized by over 7 percent of parent consolidated sales devoted to advertising, and technological innovation, measured by over 5 percent of parent sales spent for research and development. Both studies also found that corporate bargaining power increased at a certain threshold of exports, between 40 and 50 percent of subsidiary sales (Poynter) or of output (Fagre and Wells). A project's size, however, decreased corporate bargaining power, again at a certain threshold: seventy-five employees or more for Poynter or over $100 million in assets for Fagre and Wells. The larger the size of foreign firms, the more politically sensitive and visible targets they are for adverse government action.

Fagre and Wells also found that the more competitors in an industry the less bargaining power any particular firm had in government negotiations. Poynter, moreover, discovered that firms experienced significantly less government intervention if they had between 50 and 89 percent indigenous personnel in senior subsidiary positions or were more politically proactive. Conversely, firms were targeted for government intervention more often if they were in a strategic industry (natural resource based, petrochemical, transportation, communication, or steel). Moreover, these studies have been recently buttressed by research undertaken in Asia by Donald Lecraw.[11]

The major limitation of the two studies is that they focus entirely on firm characteristics and behavior. Since bargaining is a reciprocal relationship, government and country characteristics and behavior should also be considered. Four general factors are relevant in this respect. First and perhaps foremost is the attractiveness of the country or market, which can be determined in a number of ways. The firm may need natural resources that the country has in abundance; the country's market size and growth prospects could be highly attractive; the country may be an excellent export base to other countries; and infrastructure supports may be favorable. In addition, a key consideration might be comparison with the options that exist for the firm given conditions in other countries and

Figure 8
Negotiation Approach Matrix

Outcome Stakes for the Firm	High	"accommodative-appeasement" (give in)		"collaborative-integration" (work with)
	Moderate		"compromise-sharing" (horse-trade)	
	Low	"avoidant-neglect" (who cares)		"competitive-domination" (steamroll)
		Low	Moderate	High
		Relative Bargaining Power of the Firm		

the behavior of competitors. Lastly, the consistency, flexibility, and fairness of past relations with international business could be crucial in determining the market's attractiveness and the host government's bargaining power.

A second general factor in the bargaining relationship is the internal coherence of the government. If there is disunity within the government concerning how to deal with international business, a divide-and-conquer strategy is possible for the firm. The resiliency of the present government is also relevant. If political risk due to instability or electoral change is high, the bargaining power of the government is lower. Finally, the competency of government officials and negotiators should be considered. If highly competent, which is increasingly the case, government bargaining power obviously rises.

As the above discussion may imply, there is now almost universal agreement among host government officials that international business contributes net economic benefits to their societies, in spite of the political costs that multinationals bring in the form of reduced national sovereignty and control.[12] Government officials through negotiations attempt to maximize economic benefits and minimize the unavoidable political costs. Handling these negotiations in a way that results in mutually satisfactory deals and relationships is a major political challenge facing international business managers today.

A variation of the Gladwin-Walter "conflict management model" may prove a useful analytical approach to negotiations between multinational corporations and host governments.[13] The negotiation-approach matrix depicted in Figure 8 captures the essence of factors that are key to bargaining power analysis, while it is also simple and straightforward enough to be manageable.

As one can see, the conflict management modes of behavior suggested by Gladwin and Walter were used, with supplemental explanations. The two sides of the matrix, however, are not multidimensional but unidimensional. Whereas Walter and Gladwin combine outcome stakes and relative bargaining power on one side of the matrix, these two factors are opposite each other here. Although outcome stakes and relative bargaining power are interrelated, in that a firm's bargaining power goes down to some degree as the stakes or potential losses go

Figure 9
Select Cases in the Negotiation Approach Matrix

Outcome Stakes for the Firm	High	Dresser in France, 1982		Honeywell in France, 1981–82
	Moderate		Hoffmann-La Roche in UK, 1971–73	
	Low	Mobil in US, 1976–77		Dresser in US, 1982
		Low	Moderate	High
		Relative Bargaining Power of the Firm		

up, these two factors are also quite distinct and are perhaps the two most important considerations any organization has when approaching negotiations. The major determinants of firm bargaining power relative to host governments are numerous, and managerial judgment must be used to combine these variables into an overall assessment. The same is true for assessing outcome stakes.

Some case examples may illustrate the negotiation-approach matrix. In Figure 9 several firms are placed in certain cells according to their relationship with a particular government during an international business conflict. Logically, if a firm faces government pressure when its bargaining power and outcome stakes are relatively low, then the firm should avoid or ignore the problem. The conflict facing Mobil Oil Corporation in 1976–77 concerning the firm's compliance with the United Nations sanctions against Rhodesia provides an example of such a situation.

Accusations were made in Congress during the fall of 1976 that Mobil's South African subsidiary was shipping oil illegally to Rhodesia, and a U.S. Department of Treasury investigation ensued. Mobil, however, insisted that it could not provide the relevant information to the U.S. government because the South African Official Secrets Act prevented Mobil in New York from inspecting records or even questioning managers of the wholly owned subsidiary. Thus Mobil's South African affiliate refused to comply with an administrative order for information served on Mobil by the U.S. Department of Treasury. As a result, in May 1977 the Treasury Department dropped the investigation because it could not determine any violations without access to the South African subsidiary's files.[14] Mobil in New York had apparently determined that it had little power to change U.S. policy toward the U.N. sanctions, but at the same time the company perceived it had little to fear from stonewalling the U.S. government.

Dresser Industries also faced the conflicting demands of two sovereign states in the Soviet pipeline controversy. Unlike Mobil in the Rhodesian oil controversy, Dresser faced two governments that were intensely committed to their respective positions. Thus Dresser initially faced high outcome stakes vis-à-vis both the U.S. and French governments.

In June 1982 the Reagan administration imposed a retroactive embargo on U.S. shipments or exports going to Western Europe's natural gas pipeline project with the Soviet Union. The embargo was applied to contracts signed prior to the embargo and to all U.S. corporate interests, including the subsidiaries of U.S. companies. This extraterritorial extension of U.S. law under the Export Control Act was vigorously opposed by several European countries, including France, which ordered Dresser's French subsidiary in August 1982 to ship three completed compressors for the pipeline under a statute that could bring criminal penalties against Dresser France's management, all of whom were French nationals. If Dresser France complied with the French order, however, the U.S. government threatened to impose sanctions, whereby Dresser France could be barred from receiving any goods or services from U.S. companies, including its parent corporation in Dallas. By telling its French subsidiary to use its best judgment to make a decision and that the corporation would support whatever decision was made, Dresser in Dallas decided to appease the French government without overtly violating U.S. law. To no one's surprise in Dallas, the compressors were shipped within the next few days.[15]

In the Dresser Soviet pipeline case, the stakes were too high and the firm's bargaining position too weak for the subsidiary's management to risk the wrath of the French government. At the same time, Dresser management in Dallas was also helpless to influence French policy and felt their traditionally strong export business to the Eastern bloc was in jeopardy as a result of the U.S.–Western European conflict. Subtly giving in to French government demands turned out to be Dresser U.S.'s only viable option.

Once a limited embargo was imposed on Dresser France by the Reagan administration, Dresser in Dallas began to aggressively challenge the U.S. action in the courts. At that point Dresser felt it had little to lose from such a competitive posture because the sanctions had already been imposed. Dresser launched these aggressive tactics, moreover, because the company believed that it was right and had a strong legal case. Although Dresser's legal moves did not directly succeed, the sanctions were essentially lifted in the fall of 1982, starting when the United States backed down from the U.K. government concerning sanctions against a British firm.

Another U.S. company faced a strong-willed French government in 1981–82 concerning the future of the computer industry in France. When Socialist Party leader François Mitterrand was elected to the French presidency in May 1981, it was clear that Honeywell's position in its most important foreign subsidiary, Honeywell-Bull, would change. Honeywell held a 47 percent share of the French subsidiary, and the majority French partner, St. Gobain, was nationalized by the government in July 1981. By November, Honeywell and St. Gobain started negotiations concerning Honeywell's future role in the Bull subsidiary, and an unofficial deal was struck in January 1982. The agreement was essentially patterned after Honeywell's initial negotiation position of November 1981. Even though the French government delayed consummation of the agreement, it was eventually signed in May 1982.[16]

The Honeywell-French deal was one that essentially continued the collaboration and integration of operations between the two parties. Although the ten-year agreement resulted in Honeywell reducing its equity position within Bull to 19.9 percent, marketing, management, and technical collaboration would continue. France and Honeywell not only agreed to cooperative distribution arrangements for each other's products but reconfirmed the concept of exclusivity of markets as well. Bull remained the principal or sole marketing arm of Honeywell in around forty countries, including the key market of Western Europe. As a result, Bull would continue manufacturing Honeywell products in France for a licensing fee. In addition there was to be coordinated development of present and future product lines through a planning committee, which had evenly balanced membership between American and French.

Honeywell's objective in the negotiations was to maximize cooperative arrangements, while shielding the parent corporation from the large and expected operating losses of the Bull subsidiary, expected to result primarily from poor public sector management. Some sort of continued collaborative integration of Honeywell and French interests was desired by the American parent because of its high stakes and was possible because of its bargaining power. Honeywell's relatively high outcome stakes were a consequence of a long-term financial, technological, and marketing interrelationship with the French subsidiary. In 1981 Bull contributed 30 percent of Honeywell's income from computer sales. In fact 10 percent of Honeywell's computer sales went to Bull. Vital research and development synergies had been created, and Bull's research and development expenditures approximated 20 percent of Honeywell's total. Lastly, a falling out between Honeywell and the French could seriously jeopardize Honeywell's marketing position in approximately forty countries and could also cause disruptions in Honeywell's traditional markets, from which Bull had been excluded in past agreements.

At the same time, Honeywell's bargaining position was relatively high. Perhaps most importantly, Honeywell had negotiated an investment guarantee in 1975, whereby the book value of its investment was placed in an escrow account in a London bank. The French side was highly dependent on Honeywell for future technology and products, as Honeywell devoted over 5 percent of sales to research and development each year. The French also wanted to protect their traditional export markets from Honeywell competition, as nearly half of total Bull revenue was exported out of France. The French had few competitive options, whether it be the Japanese, other European firms, or U.S. companies. In short, the French government needed Honeywell to achieve its goal of creating a world-class national computer industry. Once informed of this French view within initial and informal discussions, Honeywell knew it had a strong bargaining position. The resulting agreement of May 1982 was a classic example of negotiations leading to a mutually satisfactory conclusion.

The case of Honeywell in France also illustrates another important point empirically supported in recent research by Lecraw. By looking at and surveying 153 subsidiaries from six home countries operating in five Association of Southeast Asian Nations (ASEAN) countries—Thailand, Malaysia, Singapore, Indonesia, and the Phillipines—Lecraw shows that there is a rough J-shaped relationship between percent equity ownership and industry success, that is, the lowest level of success occurs when equity ownership is more or less equally divided between the multinational and its local partners. Effective control over certain vital functions of the subsidiary, however, is linearly related to industry success. Moreover, there is not a close relationship between equity ownership and effective control. Lecraw concluded, therefore, that a multinational corporation

> may be able to retain control over the factors of the operation of its subsidiary that are important to it, even though it has a low level of equity participation. A TNC [transnational corporation] may therefore be able to reduce the level of its equity participation in response to host country demands while retaining control over the factors that are critical to the success of the investment.[17]

In effect this is what Honeywell did. Honeywell wanted a reduction in its equity position to below 20 percent not only to avoid the need to consolidate Bull's profit and loss statement on Honeywell's corporate books but to help appease certain French nationalists as well. The functions, however, that were extremely important to Honeywell were retained, namely marketing and technological collaboration.

Whereas the case of Honeywell in France illustrates a symbolic success story in international business negotiations, the case of Hoffman-LaRoche in the United Kingdom demonstrates the opposite. Hoffmann-LaRoche's negotiation strategy or conflict management approach vis-à-vis the U.K. government was fatally flawed because of a failure by corporate management in Basle to rationally assess the firms' outcome stakes and relative bargaining power. By following alternatively a neglect-ignore, then a domination-steamroll approach, while its relatively high stakes and moderate bargaining position logically dictated a compromise/sharing attitude, the company placed itself at undue risk in the United Kingdom and worldwide as well.

Under the British health care system, medicine costs resulting from prescriptions were ultimately reimbursed by the Department of Health and Social Services (DHSS). In 1967 DHSS started a Voluntary Price Regulation System for all pharmaceutical companies operating in Britain, but Hoffmann-LaRoche refused to join or to divulge any information on sales or costs. DHSS, therefore, was unable to determine if Roche's prices for Valium and Librium were warranted or reasonable by the department's definition. DHSS forced Roche to submit annual U.K. financial statements in 1970, and because of information so received and given Roche's lack of cooperation, DHSS referred the entire matter to the Monopolies Commission in 1971. In the meantime the company continued to refuse any lowering of its prices.

In April 1973 the Monopolies Commission issued its report, which was highly critical of Roche's refusal to provide information and of drastic divergence between the arms'-length prices for raw materials used in the manufacture of the company's drugs and the firm's transfer prices. The commission urged drastic cuts in Roche's Valium and Librium prices. Within two days the British Department of Trade and Industry (DTI) under a Special Order demanded that Roche reduce prices on Librium and Valium by 60 and 75 percent respectively; the Special Order was approved by the House of Commons and went into effect on April 23, 1973. A copy of the Monopoly Commissions report was also sent to the European Economic Community (EEC) Commission. Within days the German Federal Cartel Office said it was launching an official investigation of Roche's pricing policies due to the U.K. findings and the fact that Valium and Librium prices in West Germany were four times higher than in Britain. The EEC Commission itself also announced that it was investigating the situation.

Roche reacted very aggressively, after years of stonewalling the U.K. government, and immediately appealed the price-cut order. On April 24 the company received leave to petition the case to the House of Lords. On the next day Roche launched a public relations blitz in the *Financial Times*, where the company strongly defended its pricing policies and actions vis-à-vis the U.K. government. This was followed by Roche's first-ever public news conference in late April 1973, headed by the company's top manager, who criticized the U.K. government by saying: "It has issued special rules with regard to just one company, thereby establishing a kind of special decree to one entity among many forming the pharmaceutical industry. We consider this a lack of fair play against which we shall fight."[18]

What Roche failed to understand was that special rules directed at select or individual companies had nothing to do with fair play and was simply a fact of life in international business. The management task is to determine the best way to cope with such legal-governmental risks in light of the particular circumstances of the situation. In Roche's case the outcome stakes were relatively high. Within the United Kingdom itself, Valium and Librium constituted almost three-quarters of the company's total sales in the country. Roche's U.K. business, moreover, contributed 3.7 percent of global sales and 7.1 percent of worldwide profit. Roche's noncooperative, aggressive stance in Britain also heightened the probability of not only angering the U.K. government but of bringing global attention to an increasingly nasty public dispute. A global-ripple effect could be disastrous since the two drugs contributed nearly half of Roche's worldwide sales.

Roche's bargaining power was also moderate at best. The company's greatest bargaining asset was the high level of research and development required in a competitive pharmaceutical firm. Roche, in fact, spent nearly 12 percent of sales on research and development each year. The firm was also a modest exporter from the United Kingdom, with exports having increased from 24 to 28 percent of its U.K. sales in recent years. A number of factors weighed against the company's bargaining power, however. First, the company's size, industry, and initial monopoly position made Roche very politically sensitive to the U.K.

government. In addition the forced licensing of Valium and Librium in 1970 to two British firms had increased competitive options for the government, reducing Roche's bargaining position. Perhaps most importantly, Roche's management of the situation since 1967 had created an adversarial, distrusting atmosphere that made future compromise difficult, if not impossible.

The company suffered for its ignorance or miscalculation of its position. In 1975 Roche and the DTI reached an out-of-court settlement, whereby Roche agreed to repay $7.7 million, due to excessive profits and monopolistic pricing. In addition the company joined the Voluntary Price Regulation System, a move that had already been preceded by the first-ever publication of corporate consolidated financial statements in 1974. The EEC Commission also ruled against Roche in 1976, leading to a fine of DM 1.1 million and to a toughening of EEC competition laws on multinationals. In effect, Roche had been forced to compromise and adapt itself to government demands in a way that led to "the almost total transformation of Roche from an enterprise uniquely secretive even for a Swiss company into a more or less responsible, open multinational corporation."[19]

Roche, therefore, in the U.K. controversy had violated almost every negotiation guideline.[20] It refused to take a compromise/sharing approach at the outset; it sought a nonzero sum-game solution instead of trying to find mutually satisfactory agreements. Roche also failed to empathize with the other side by understanding a government's need to balance economic benefits with political costs when dealing with multinationals. The firm, moreover, escalated and intensified the confrontation when its chairman held the company's first press conference. In general public intervention in a dispute with a host government should be avoided. Lastly, there was no evidence that Roche had undertaken any interdependent or contingency decision making. Their behavior instead was one of hostile reaction. Whereas openly hostile activity is recommended for certain limited situations, a reactive mode of behavior is never wise. A firm should instead objectively assess its stakes and relative bargaining position and make contingency plans accordingly.

The selective intervention of governments against individual companies has, of course, become more widespread and institutionalized around the world since the Hoffmann-LaRoche case in the United Kingdom. In fact governmental-legal political risk is more prevalent and important than extra-legal risk today. Usually, such forms of government intervention against multinational firms are preceded by or implemented within a negotiation framework. International business, therefore, needs conceptual guidance and general rules of behavior when faced with such situations, as indicated in the negotiation-approach matrix.

PORTFOLIO PLANNING AND POLITICAL RISK MANAGEMENT

The traditional way of integrating political risk forecasts into corporate decision making was a quasi-portfolio approach that viewed the company's various international operations and opportunities in a matrix format, comparing the ventures' attractiveness against situations of high and low political risk.[21] An interpretive synthesis of how multinational corporations used such a matrix is presented in Figure 10. In the matrix it is assumed that the more attractive a country or market, the more willing a firm will be to chance a higher likelihood of political risk. Firms operating in a large and fast-growing market, however, will vary their organizational structure and financial exposure according to the degree of political risk. In a highly attractive but politically risky country, companies will suboptimalize their market performance or profits through joint venture or nonequity arrangements. In game theory this is similar to a "minimax" strategy. Firms in attractive markets with low political risk probabilities, on the other hand, prefer to optimalize profits and market position through wholly owned subsidiaries, but in such situations they will adapt to host government pressures or preferences if necessary. Conversely, firms should avoid weak markets with a high likelihood of political risk. Such situations are also subject to divestment or to a low level of business activity through export sales agents or limited licensing agreements. Relatively unattractive markets in countries with low political risk potential, however, are subject to slightly more business activity, with export sales possibly handled through a formal distribution system and fixed investments usually subject to joint venture arrangements.

Such an approach to political risk management has three major drawbacks. First, it does not directly address firm characteristics. This omission makes the critical task of bargaining power analysis very difficult. Second, industry and competitive factors are largely ignored, which also impacts on a firm's bargaining position. Lastly, a firm's tactics as an influence on the external environment are not addressed. The traditional matrix instead implicitly assumes the firm to be a passive, reactive agent. Such an assumption ignores many possible risk-management approaches and alternatives.

The generalizations contained in this matrix, however, can be used as starting points for a more sophisticated and comprehensive integration of political risk into corporate decision making. The notion of venture attractiveness can be replaced by strategic business unit (SBU) or portfolio concepts. In effect venture attractiveness can be broken down into various subcomponents (market growth rate, market size, ROI, strategic fit), with a composite ranking then plotted against the firm's overall competitive position (relative market share, managerial-organizational capabilities, profitability, cash flow position, market fit, etc.). Highly attractive markets with strong competitive positions can be considered "Stars." The opposite situations (low attraction, weak competitive position) are "Dogs." On the other hand, an SBU that is a strong competitor in a previously attractive but declining market is a big potential generator of funds to the corporate portfolio; thus it is a "Cash Cow." Conversely, an SBU with a weak competitive position in a booming or growing market is a "Problem Child" that needs a lot of cash if market share is to increase. A comparison of the SBU categorization with the level (probability) and type of political risk can help

Figure 10
Venture Attraction–Political Risk Matrix

<u>Spread/Share Risk</u>

(1) <u>Participation Mode:</u>
- a. Joint venture preferred, esp. employee ownership scheme
- b. non-equity arrangements if suitable (license)

H (2) <u>Financial:</u>
- a. insurance coverage
- b. borrow over equity (local or "trans-national alliances")
- c. seek investment guarantees from host government

(3) <u>Operational:</u>
- a. control or scrutinize parent to subsidiary technology transfers
- b. maximize expatriate managers in key positions

(4) <u>Political:</u>
- a. avoid host government alliances/contacts
- b. maintain low profile

<u>Adaptation/Integratism</u>

(1) <u>Participation Mode:</u>
- a. wholly owned subsidiary preferred
- b. joint venture is necessary

(2) <u>Financial:</u>
- a. external over local (debt or equity)
- b. local over external procurement

(3) <u>Operational:</u>
- a. maximize technology transfers
- b. maximize role of local managers
- c. create local Board of Directors

(4) <u>Political:</u>
- a. seek host government alliances
- b. maintain high profile as good corporate citizen

Venture Attractiveness

L

Avoidance/Hedge Risk

(1) Participation Mode

a. limited exporting, licensing arrangements preferred
b. total avoidance, divestment strong possibility
c. equity position unlikely unless subsidiary is part of an integrated sourcing system

(2) Financial:

a. if occasional exporting, confirmed letters of credit
b. if licensing, higher, up-front, fixed fees
c. if equity, insurance, and high, quick capital
c. outflow

(3) Operational:

a. limit technology/skill transfers
b. maximize expatriates in key positions
c. diversification a possible consideration

(4) Political:

a. low public profile
b. selective coalition-building

Internal Indifference/External Motivations

(1) Participation Mode:

a. export/investment intensity/volume highly related to competitors' behavior
b. Local production presence highly related to global sourcing strategy

(2) Financial:

a. flexible, more standard contracts
b. limited financial commitment as a percentage of total corporate assets

(3) Operational:

a. if significant export, investment presence, maximize local managers or minimize commitments of expatriates
b. if production, maximize technology transfers

(4) Political:

a. seek alliances
b. high profile

H — Degrees of Political Risk — L

shape strategic decision making. In fact there appears to be strong empirical evidence that this approach to political risk management is becoming more popular among large U.S.-based multinational corporations during the last few years. An interpretive composite of how portfolio or SBU-based planning and political risk are integrated by these U.S. firms is depicted in Figure 11.

Six case studies can more clearly demonstrate how the linkage between portfolio planning and political risk analysis might be specifically interpreted. Two of the firms studied, GTE and Itek, entered export-service contracts with Iran during the 1970s. GTE in 1977 signed one of the largest telecommunications contracts in history, while Itek sold under $30 million worth of high technology, defense-related reconnaissance equipment in the same year. GTE had operated in the country since the 1950s and felt, based on their experience, the political environment was relatively safe and certain. Itek, however, had never operated in this or any other Middle Eastern country. Their apprehension about an uncertain political environment was relatively high. Moreover, trips to the country by top executives exposed them to incidents that heightened their fears of a politically risky situation.

Regardless of their different risk perceptions, both companies were fully committed to their respective and lucrative contracts, but GTE, unlike Itek, did virtually nothing to reduce its financial exposure. Political risk tactics used to protect what we could consider Itek's Star contract were varied and included extensive insurance coverage, a faster rate of return (accomplished by demanding a larger down payment than normal during final contract negotiations), and extensive contingency planning.

These efforts proved fruitful after the Iranian revolution occurred. Insurance payments have or will net the company $2.5 million; the higher down payment increased in-hand revenues by over $1.5 million; and contingency planning allowed the firm to act quickly within the U.S. legal system to stop the payment of letters of credit, which had been issued to the former government as a security guarantee of its performance, and to attach property (airplanes) owned by Iran but physically located in the U.S. No other firm of the several hundred operating in the country before the governmental change is known to have been able to obtain a similar court injunction or property attachment.

GTE seems to have reacted to the traumatic events in a relatively passive, fatalistic manner, even though inattention to political risk considerations had exposed them to around $60 million in after-tax losses. A continued inattention has been evident in a lack of stress on these kinds of issues at both the corporate- and line-management levels and in a relatively mechanical, uncoordinated approach toward country risk analysis as well. The country risk analysis that is done takes on a strongly quantitative aspect, which is overwhelmingly dominated by econometric modeling, and appears to be diffused, with such responsibility having been dispersed among three separate locations. Although within the last two years an attempt has been made to focus a major portion of that responsibility in one place, by creating a vice president for international affairs, this person acts as a lone troubleshooter for foreign operations.

The difficulty that this kind of approach might engender was perhaps illustrated by a recent development for GTE in Brazil. The Brazilian government, which has a long history of selective intervention and strategic industry protection, forced GTE, in 1982, to sell enough shares of its wholly owned subsidiary to gain national majority equity ownership and control. The terms of the induced sale were reported to be adverse to the multinational corporation. A more proactive stance might have produced a more beneficial result.

Dow Chemical faced the possibility of forced divestment in the same country because it also operates a wholly owned subsidiary in a strategic industry. Unlike GTE, however, Dow had an extremely proactive approach toward the political environment and had focused the country risk analysis function in one corporate location. Its risk assessment unit constantly monitored various investment climates in a highly systematic, qualitative manner and then reported their findings directly to the chairman of the board.

Their political risk evaluation of the project in Brazil was that a high probability of adverse government intervention existed. Reasons for this evaluation included: a history of active government intervention against foreign subsidiaries that were wholly owned; local and government capacity in petrochemical production rapidly increasing as new plants came on stream; Dow's strong coalition supporter (a former leader of the country and a past president of their local subsidiary) was now quite old; the technological superiority of the firm was dwindling due to the local presence of a large national research and development effort (over two hundred researchers, fewer than five of whom were expatriate); the company exported very little if any of its production; and public opinion surveys indicated the younger, more educated and media-influenced population favored highly restrictive policies toward foreign investment.

At the same time, the market attractiveness of Brazil was very high. Dow was a market-share leader in the full line of petrochemicals produced, and growth prospects in this large market were greater than nearly all alternatives worldwide. The firm thus perceived its subsidiary to be a Star investment. The recommendation to top management by their chief political risk analyst was to seek a joint venture partner on favorable terms before the government dictated their options to them. Such a preemptive strategy seems highly appropriate for a Star investment in a very threatening political environment.

The last Star SBU to be discussed concerns IBM France. When the Mitterrand government was elected in 1981, its stated intention was to create an autonomous, competitive computer industry that was government controlled. Apparently to facilitate this long-range strategy, the government renegotiated an agreement with Honeywell concerning the Bull joint venture. IBM's wholly owned subsidiary, however, was under no immediate threat from this partnership because of its relative size and rationalized production techniques. In other words, IBM

Figure 11
SBU—Political Risk Matrix

H	(1) Participation Mode: a. Joint venture if bargaining power weak b. Wholly owned subsidiary if bargaining power strong	(1) Participation Mode: a. Usually avoid or divest b. If extra-legal risk low, joint venture and/or license deal possible	(1) Participation Mode: a. If feasible, management service contract when extra legal risk is high and/or bargaining power weak	(1) Participation Mode: a. Avoid or divest in nearly all cases b. Limited exporting or license possible c. Equity only if integrated sourcing plant
	(2) Financial: a. Insurance necessary if bargaining power weak b. Borrow over equity if bargaining power weak c. Consider equity carrot if bargaining power strong	(2) Financial: a. Minimize capital inflows b. Local over external financing c. Insurance, if equity	(2) Financial: a. Insurance if equity position maintained b. Maximize size and speed of capital outflows	(2) Financial: a. Maximize capital outflow and insurance if equity b. Confirmed letters of credit if exporting c. High, up-front, fixed fees if licensing
	(3) Operational: a. Relate technology transfer policy to impact on bargaining power b. Relate management policy to bargaining power	(3) Operational: a. Relate technology/management policies to bargaining power b. But tendency to maximize technology transfers if integrated sourcing plant	(3) Operational: a. Relate technology transfer policy to bargaining power b. Relate management policy to bargaining power	(3) Operational: a. Minimize technology, skill transfers b. If extra-legal risk low, diversification perhaps
	(4) Political: a. Avoid formal government alliances if extra-legal risk high b. Maximize informal contacts in and outside government if bargaining power high regardless of risk type c. Maximize low public profile	(4) Political: a. Maximize informal contacts b. Maximize low public profile	(4) Political: a. Seek select government allies (finance) b. Low public profile	(4) Political: a. Selective allies b. Low public profile

ENVIRONMENTAL POLITICAL RISK

(1) <u>Participation Mode:</u>
- a. Wholly owned subsidiary preferred
- b. If government pressure and bargaining power weak, then joint venture

(2) <u>Financial:</u>
- a. External over local financing
- b. Local over external procurement

(3) <u>Operational:</u>
- a. Relate technology transfers to impact on bargaining power if government pressure or objections
- b. Maximize technology transfers if no government pressure
- c. Same for management policy

(4) <u>Political:</u>
- a. Seek government allies
- b. Maintain high public profile

STAR

(1) <u>Participation Mode:</u>
- a. Joint venture preferred if market commercially acceptable
- b. Wholly owned subsidiary perhaps if cash-rich and no government pressure that is significant

(2) <u>Financial:</u>
- a. Minimize capital inflows and maximize local financing if joint venture
- b. Maximize capital inflows if wholly owned

(3) <u>Operational:</u>
- a. Maximize technology transfers in most cases
- b. Balanced management team between locals and expatriates

(4) <u>Political:</u>
- a. Seek allies
- b. High public profile

PROBLEM CHILD

(1) <u>Participation Mode:</u>
- a. Wholly owned subsidiary preferred
- b. If government pressure and bargaining power weak, mgt. service over joint pressure

(2) <u>Financial:</u>
- a. Insurance if equity position maintained
- b. Maximize size and speed capital outflows

(3) <u>Operational:</u>
- a. Relate technology/management policies in bargaining power if government pressure
- b. Maximize technology transfers and local management if no government pressure

(4) <u>Political:</u>
- a. Seek allies
- b. High public profile

CASH COW

(1) <u>Participation Mode:</u>
- a. Export, business actively related to competitor's behavior
- b. Local production presence related to sourcing system

(2) <u>Financial:</u>
- a. Flexible, standard contracts
- b. Limited financial exposure

(3) <u>Operational:</u>
- a. If export, marketing minimize expatriates
- b. If production, maximize technology transfers

(4) <u>Political:</u>
- a. Seek allies
- b. High public profile

DOG

France employed thousands of workers, and the local plants were not full production lines but only part of a European-wide system of production. Over time, however, top management could forecast a possible ''falling Star'' based on the following factors: government intentions in the computer field (strongly supported by the main opposition party); the creation of the new joint-venture previously mentioned; and the government's role as the largest customer and contributor to the firm's dominant market share position within France. Given the possibility of IBM France moving from a Star to a Cash Cow during the next five to ten years, contingency plans for a very slow and measured harvest could prove fruitful. This, however, was only one major contingency, for IBM obviously would prefer to maintain the French subsidiary's Star position and would try to do so if at all possible. In that connection the company negotiated understandings with the government to help the French restructure their computer industry. IBM apparently hoped that such negotiations would help them maintain or increase their market position.

The strategic view of Honeywell in the same market was quite different. IBM France's market share was several times larger than the one held by Honeywell through their Bull subsidiary. At the same time, growth prospects in the computer field were very high, and market size was the largest in the world due to the Common Market trade structure. Honeywell-Bull, therefore, was positioned as a classic Problem Child.

In approximately 90 percent of all Problem-Child situations, a firm decides not to risk the large infusion of funds necessary to substantially increase market share, regardless of the political risk climate. After the Mitterrand election, the legal-government risk faced by Honeywell was very threatening and uncertain. As a result, their initial position was to completely sell their minority equity of shares based on a predetermined and legally binding price, negotiated five years earlier due to the company's fear of future government intervention in the computer industry. This total sellout or withdrawal tactic completely conforms to past indications of what a manager should do with a Problem Child in a high risk country.

The French government, however, given its long-range strategy, wanted Honeywell to remain an equity partner in Bull, preferably at their present level of 47 percent. Terms were then negotiated which gave Honeywell substantial incentives to remain in the joint venture. First, their equity share was decreased to 19.9 percent and sold at bonus prices when compared to the terms of the binding contract. Their equity level was reduced low enough, moreover, to allow the firm to avoid reporting expected and large near-term losses of the Bull subsidiary on their consolidated balance sheet. Second, technology transfer agreements were signed that would result in large royalty payments to Honeywell in the next few years. Third, any technology breakthroughs based on transferred technology were automatically accessible to Honeywell. Fourth, France committed itself to the infusion of billions of dollars in the joint venture for product development and market expansion.

In short Honeywell negotiated an ideal arrangement for an expansionary Problem Child strategy. Little capital was at risk in a major and difficult market share battle with a large and powerful competitor. At the same time, even if the French expansion effort was only partially successful, Honeywell would still reap many benefits—lucrative royalties, a technology supplier, and the undermining and siphoning of resources away from its major competitor in that and other markets.

A final case study involves General Electric (GE), which had investments in four product groups in South Africa. Each of the above product groups were identical to SBUs, which heavily influenced this firm's planning process. During the crisis that accompanied the 1976 Soweto riots, an in-depth, qualitative country study was undertaken by corporate staff in close interaction with line management.

The resulting report posited two main scenarios about the ''macro'' environment. The most likely scenario was assigned a 50 percent probability, and it included a sociopolitical and economic forecast for the country as a whole. In general the forecast was characterized as ''moderately unfavorable'' because the sociopolitical environment would be ''relatively unstable,'' even though not leading to a change in government, and economic growth would be slightly below historic patterns. The second most likely scenario was given a 40 percent likelihood and would result in a ''moderately favorable'' environment. Socially and politically, the country would be ''relatively stable,'' and the economy would be fairly ''healthy and prosperous.''

Each of these macro forecasts were applied to each product group or SBU, in effect addressing the ''micro'' or product-specific risks and opportunities that GE faced in South Africa. Product Group A was considered borderline ''Cash Cow—Dog,'' and in the most likely scenario, a significant decrease in that product's growth and market share position would be experienced. At the same time, the level of political risk was considered moderately high. A harvest or gradual withdrawal recommendation was given if this scenario developed.

The harvest or ''milk'' option, however, was only one major possibility. If the moderately favorable scenario developed, for example, Product Group A's market share position should be maintained and growth rates should decline only slightly. This product group, moreover, would face only a moderate to low political risk. As a result, a ''protect'' or maintain recommendation was made for the second scenario, which in fact occurred after this report was completed.

In Product Group B the two scenarios put less importance on the micro political risk environment and thus on strategic recommendations. Growth rates and profit margins for this classic Cash Cow would be slightly less in the most likely scenario relative to the second most likely, but they were acceptable in either case. Consequently, a maintain or protect recommendation was given regardless of which scenario developed.

The same situation existed for Product Group C. In both scenarios growth rates would be high and profits attractive. This Star SBU faced low political risk in either case. Thus an invest-and-grow recommendation was made for both scenarios.

In the fourth product group the recommended strategic response varied dramatically under the two scenarios. This SBU was considered a classic Problem Child. Although the political risk level was low in each scenario, growth and profit prospects differed significantly. In the most likely scenario, a policy of selective divestment was recommended because growth rates for these products would decline and inadequate profits would be encountered. In the second scenario, however, growth rates would exceed the national average, and profit margins would reach a very acceptable or "reasonable" level. A strategic recommendation of "selective emphasis" naturally followed. In terms of contingencies, areas of selective emphasis were determined before it was known which scenario would occur so as not to preclude any future options. That is, under a temporary economic downturn, one did not want to begin divesting those product lines that would be targets for an invest-and-grow emphasis when and if the economy rebounded.

The SBU-political risk matrix has a number of advantages over the traditional decision-making guidelines depicted in Figure 9. First, the integration of political risk within an SBU framework leads to a more comprehensive treatment of relevant variables. In addition the key consideration of bargaining power analysis takes a central role. This approach also facilitates scenario development and contingency planning. Perhaps most important, however, political risk analysis based on a portfolio-planning system tends to maximize input from line management, thus increasing the firm's chances of correctly implementing its strategic political risk objectives. Finally, as the GE case demonstrates, the primary value of SBU-political risk integration is the facilitation of comparative investment analysis. Although in the GE case this related to different product types in the same country, this kind of investment analysis might be even more valuable when comparing product or project risks across countries.

MANAGERIAL IMPLICATIONS AND CONCLUSIONS

Scenario development and contingency planning is a fundamental step in sound international business management. In dealing with today's complex, turbulent, and uncertain environment, only a range of possible developments can be predicted reasonably. However, no more than two to three scenarios should undergo intensive analysis because of the need for manageability. Interrelationships between scenarios should also be studied. This approach amounts to proactive analysis and planning. Chapter 6 will discuss scenario planning in greater detail.

Such observations strongly imply that one's approach to the strategic integration of political risk can never be mechanical. Abstract, theoretical guidelines or tendencies can be posited, but they should not be viewed as automatic prescriptions for action. For example, Star ventures facing high political risks are not automatically subject to joint venture formation or other risk-sharing tactics. In particular, and depending on the probability and type of political risk faced under different scenarios, a firm with a Star SBU may still be able to remain a wholly owned subsidiary. Similarly, the bargaining strengths and characteristics of the firm will also affect the viability of different ownership levels and modes of participation in foreign countries.

In essence every investment-management decision is unique, although comparability between different situations is possible. Managers should automatically study each problem with an eye on both past experience for guidance and on the particular aspects of the present problem that deviate from precedent.

Another observation concerns the importance of perceptions in political risk analysis and related decisions. As the GTE and Itek cases in Iran demonstrated, only perceptions are acted upon, and if political risk analysis is handled passively or inadvertently, preconceptions will dictate political risk forecasts. In turbulent environments operating on the basis of preconceived assumptions (or only on the simple extrapolation of past trends into future) is dangerous and foolhardy. A proactive, scenario-building approach that constantly challenges preconceptions is the more successful tactic.

Legal-governmental acts are the most pervasive political risk threats to international business today. Revolutionary change is a fairly extraordinary political risk threat, while changes in laws or regulations targeted at specific companies or industries are increasingly common. Politically proactive firms are particularly rewarded in high legal-governmental risk environments. In such situations micro risk dominates and is firm-specific. In high extra-legal risk environments macro risk, which largely affects all firms equally, is more likely and is less conducive to tactical responses.

In terms of the organization of political risk analysis, it seems to matter little where the focal responsibility for such analysis is located. Although there is a strong tendency to place political risk analysts in or close to the planning function, firms which have instead viewed such responsibility as an integral and critical part of top management's job can claim a great deal of success in this area as well. Thus, the key to the successful integration of political risk analysis into strategy is not the organizational location of the analysis but more the stress and importance attached to this kind of activity. In the final analysis the chief executive officer is usually needed to set the tone for the proper nurturing of a political risk management culture.

NOTES

1. Manfred Halpern, "The Rate and Costs of Political Development," *Annals*, 358, 1965, pp. 20–28; Samuel P. Huntington, "The Change to Change: Modernization, Development, and Politics," *Comparative Politics*, April 1971, pp. 283–322; and James A. Bill and Robert L. Hardgrave, Jr., *Comparative Politics: The Quest for Theory* (Columbus: Charles E. Merrill Publishing Company, 1973), pp. 66–83.

2. Samuel P. Huntington, *Political Order in Changing Societies* (New Haven: Yale University Press, 1972), pp. 12–24.

3. For an excellent discussion of political participation, see Myron Weiner, "Political Participation: Crisis of the Political Process," *Crises and Sequences in Political Devel-*

opment, Leonard Binder, *et al.* (Princeton: Princeton University Press, 1971), pp. 159–204.

4. Amir Taheri, quoted by James A. Bill, "Iran and the Crisis of '78," *Foreign Affairs*, Winter 1978–79, p. 330.

5. Marion Levy, *Modernization and the Structure of Societies* (Princeton: Princeton University Press, 1966), pp. 35–36.

6. Charles R. Kennedy, Jr., *The Politics of Agricultural Modernization: A Comparative Study of Land Reform in Pakistan, India, Japan and Iran*, Ph.D. dissertation, University of Texas at Austin, 1980, pp. 1–23.

7. Thomas A. Poynter, "Strategic Response to Government Intervention in Developing Countries," *Political Risks in International Business: New Directions for Research, Management, and Public Policy*, Thomas L. Brewer, ed. (New York: Praeger Publishers, 1985), p. 265.

8. Ibid., p. 262.

9. Donald J. Lecraw, "Bargaining Power, Ownership, and Profitability of Transnational Corporations in Developing Countries," *Journal of International Business Studies*, Spring-Summer 1984, p. 28.

10. Thomas A. Poynter, "Government Intervention in Less Developed Countries: The Experience of Multinational Companies," *Journal of International Business Studies*, Spring-Summer 1982, pp. 9–25; and Nathan Fagre and Louis T. Wells, "Bargaining Power of Multinationals and Host Governments," *Journal of International Business Studies*, Fall 1982, pp. 9–23.

11. Lecraw, "Bargaining Power, Ownership, and Profitability," pp. 35–41.

12. Joseph La Palombara and Stephen Blank, *Multinational Corporations and National Elites: A Study in Tensions* (New York: The Conference Board, 1976), pp. 5–6; and Joseph La Palombara and Stephen Blank, *Multinational Corporations and Developing Countries* (New York: The Conference Board, 1979), pp. 68–84.

13. Thomas Gladwin and Ingo Walter, *Multinationals Under Fire: Lessons in the Management of Conflict* (New York: John Wiley and Sons, 1980), pp. 66–89.

14. Ibid., pp. 178–80.

15. See the Colgate Darden Graduate School of Business case, *Dresser and the Soviet Pipeline*, Charles R. Kennedy, Jr., forthcoming.

16. See the Colgate Darden Graduate School of Business case, *Honeywell in France*, Charles R. Kennedy, Jr., UVA-BP-234, 1984.

17. Lecraw, "Bargaining Power, Ownership, and Profitability," pp. 39–40.

18. See Harvard Business School case, *F. Hoffman-La Roche & Co. A. G.*, James Leonhard, 9-374-201, 1974.

19. Gladwin and Walter, *Multinationals Under Fire*, pp. 350–53.

20. John Fayerweather and Ashok Kapoor, *Strategy and Negotiation for the International Corporation: Guidelines and Cases* (Cambridge: Ballinger, 1976), pp. 29–49.

21. José De La Torre, "Foreign Investment and Economics Development: Conflict and Negotiation," *Journal of International Business Studies*, Fall 1981, pp. 11–13; and see Harvard Business School note *Political Forecasting as a Management Tool*, James Austin and David Yoffie, July 1982, p. 16.

6

Future Directions

The management of political and country risk by both international banks and nonfinancial multinationals will become a more complex and higher-stakes game in the future. It will be more complex because, in all likelihood, general business exposure will spread to more and more countries, interdependencies among these countries will increase, turbulence within many countries will rise, and strategic planning uncertainties for corporations will mount as a result. The stakes will be higher because of greater absolute levels of exposure, driven by the competitive need to go abroad and enhanced involuntary lending, and because political risk management will have a major competitive impact on firms.

Given the complexity, uncertainty, and higher stakes, the adoption of sophisticated scenario development techniques in the corporate decision-making process is crucial. Scenarios are designed to deal with highly complex and uncertain issues. They also provide the basis for strategic contingency planning. Only through such techniques can one best protect and manage a highly diversified and large international portfolio.

In scenario development, alternative futures are derived from the vantage point of the issue or problem being faced by the firm. In other words scenario development should be decision oriented. In developing scenarios for both international banks and nonfinancial multinationals, one faces at least two separate sets of problems or issues. As noted in Chapter 5, the relevant focus or area of most concern for lenders versus investors is dramatically different. Banks will be more concerned with the short-term, balance-of-payment and macroeconomic situation; nonfinancial multinationals are more interested in long-term societal trends.

Reflecting these different interests, the following discussion of scenarios will treat banks and industrial, manufacturing firms separately. Therefore, the primary issue or problem that grounds the scenario development exercise for banks concerns prospects for the international debt crisis. For nonfinancial multinationals, on the other hand, the interests of companies are far too varied to readily follow such a unidimensional or single event-oriented analysis. Despite the diversity of industrial interests, however, all foreign direct investors have a common concern for the future role of multinational corporations in the evolving global political economy. For this reason, scenarios that project the general state of the international investment climate will also be a central part of this chapter. These two scenario exercises are undertaken because they highlight the importance of a strategic focus on political economy and will drive the overall, long-range direction of international banking and business. International banks and multinational corporations, moreover, can influence the way these scenarios develop and impact their interests.

SCENARIO DEVELOPMENT

Scenarios were first developed for military planning by researchers at the Rand Corporation during the 1950s.[1] Scenario development, however, was not used extensively in U.S. corporations until the 1970s, when single-line or trend forecasts had proven unreliable during times of environmental turbulence. As P. W. Beck, planning director of Shell U.K., Ltd., observed,

> The 1950s and 1960s were marked by a growing belief that the future could be made more certain through increasingly sophisticated systems of analysis, data gathering and processing, leading to greater control. The events of the 1970s have undermined this belief, and thus the future appears to be comparatively more uncertain against this former certainty that the future could be predicted and controlled.[2]

In the face of this increased uncertainty, scenario planning became more and more popular, most of all initially with capital-intensive industries like petroleum, which invested in projects with very long lead times.[3] Greater uncertainty, on top of a ten- or fifteen-year perspective, naturally propelled top oil executives toward scenario development. By 1978, however, the use of scenarios had obviously spread to more and more industries, as over a quarter of a 196-firm sample employed scenario development.[4] Banks were also big users of scenarios: a 1981 study of eleven major banks showed 55 percent of them utilized a scenario-development approach.[5] Planning on the basis of scenarios is expected to become even more important and widespread among corporations in the future.

A recommended approach to scenario development involves six discrete steps.[6] First, the firm's business-specific interests need to be explicitly selected and prioritized. It is best to identify the key issue or common cluster of issues that most critically grounds the scenario development exercise for the firm. To a large extent, the exact issue focus chosen will depend on temporal and spatial considerations. For example, a medium- or long-term perspective on global political economy leads international banks to concentrate on prospects for the international debt crisis. On the other hand, a specific loan or country exposure limit proposal may dictate a shorter-term perspective on a more country-specific basis. Of course, the interaction between such global and country scenarios is important to consider as well.

After issue identification, one selects the key environmental influences or drivers that will impact business-specific interests. The selection of drivers is a critical step in scenario development, for without a great deal of accuracy in their selection, scenarios will not properly represent or encapsulate the future and will not be of much value. Drivers by their very role in the process largely dictate the scope and direction of subsequent analysis. In effect they are the independent variables that will influence the dependent variables of business-specific interests; they should be chosen with that always in mind. A driver should meet two important conditions: a direct and significant impact on business interests and a substantial degree of autonomous force on those interests.

In order to choose the right drivers accurately, one must undertake an extensive analysis of past and present relationships. Employing the conceptual framework of political economy, discussed earlier, might prove to be quite useful in this connection. As the Bankers Trust vice president who headed the Political Assessment Group observed,

> The first phase [of scenario development] is a period of careful study of the history of the situation and of present relationships. No projection into the future can aspire to validity unless it is rooted in an understanding of the past as well as the present.[7]

The third step in scenario development, equally dependent on that extensive and detailed analysis, involves the projection of driver outcomes. Each driver should have two or three contending projections. A key consideration here is to ensure that the various driver outcomes are reasonable and internally consistent when they are combined to form scenarios. For example, if one has two drivers, such as world oil prices and global GNP growth rates, it would be unreasonable to project rapidly rising oil prices in the midst of a strong and long-term economic expansion.

The fourth step, therefore, is the combining of drivers into scenarios. This step, of course, naturally flows from or is part of the process of projecting driver outcomes. As a Conoco memorandum stated, there is no discrete step in scenario development in which the drivers are combined. Instead, this step acts as a convenient point for checking that the drivers' outcomes provide a satisfactory range of possible futures and that they are both internally consistent and plausible.[8]

The fifth step is the strategic assessment of scenarios. One must project the consequences that each scenario has on business-specific interests. The relative probability of different scenarios should usually be made explicit. How the firm can affect the development of different scenarios, or their probabilities of occurring, should be considered as well.

At that point, top management has certain options as to how to respond strategically or plan for scenarios, the final step in the process. Optimally, one strategy can be found that is best for all possible scenarios. Often, however, managers will face situations where different strategies will be optimal in various scenarios. In such cases top management can develop strategies that maximize gain for most scenarios, while at the same time minimizing risk. Alternatively, a strategy that gambles on the development of a certain scenario may be chosen, especially if a single scenario totally dominates the possibilities or if the benefits of guessing right far outweigh the costs of guessing wrong. Of course, if top management has the temperament and values of a riverboat gambler, then such a single-minded strategy is even more likely.[9]

In general, however, prudent and wise management precludes such an approach. One should always maximize options. Contingency planning serves this purpose. Even if a single scenario dominates the possibilities, trigger events or a list of leading indicators can still be developed and monitored. Strategy can then be sequenced to fit developments. Such a strategic contingency approach is particularly important when no scenario is dominant and when no strategy is best for all possible outcomes.[10]

SCENARIOS FOR THE INTERNATIONAL DEBT CRISIS

The beginning of the international debt crisis can be traced symbolically to the Mexican government's announcement in August 1982 that it could no longer repay international loans on time. As Leopoldo Solis, economic adviser to President de la Madrid, admitted, this move by Mexico had multiple motives.

> In addition to recognizing officially a *de facto* situation, the announcement was aimed at initiating a process whereby the maturities of the debt—those that remained for 1982, 1983, and 1984—would be restructured. It was also sought to persuade the private banks which were creditors of the public sector to commit themselves to continue lending to Mexico during her period of economic adjustment (1983–85). The decision to force the negotiation with international banks formed part of a concerted set of acts directed towards a credit agreement with the IMF.[11]

In many respects, the strategy outlined by Solis, that of forcing more money from commercial banks through negotiations with the IMF, succeeded. The concept and fact of involuntary lending arose and spread to the rescheduling agreements of other debtor countries. Of course, the term "involuntary lending" most aptly applies to the smaller regional banks rather than the nine major-money-center banks. As Morgan Guaranty Trust Company said,

> Virtually all large international banks realize that it is in their best interest to continue to work closely with the borrowing countries toward a solution to their debt problem. However, some of the smaller or regional banks—many in the United States as well as some abroad—have a different perspective. They have relatively small exposures and often no interest in continuing to do business with some

countries. Even if they can be persuaded to roll over existing loans, they are loath to advance any new money.[12]

In spite of this reluctance, most regional banks along with major-money-center banks have advanced substantial sums of new money to the debtor countries. As a result of the process that started with the Mexican-IMF agreement of November 1982, the Bank for International Settlements (BIS) reported that bank claims on the ten major debtors (Argentina, Brazil, Chile, Ecuador, Mexico, Peru, Venezuela, Philippines, Nigeria, and Yugoslavia) rose $9.7 billion between the end of 1982 and March 1985. This net rise in new lending largely involved a pro rata calculation of existing creditors' exposure in each country. In fact this procedure resulted in more than $24 billion in new money being disbursed between 1983 and 1985, with most of this sum being used to repay old loans or to cover net declines in trade credits and interbank lines. Consequently, total outstanding debt to these ten countries stood at $256 billion by March 1985. Total bank claims on all developing countries rose, as well, to $451 billion.[13]

The most important business-related interest of international banks, therefore, concerns prospects for the international debt crisis. As the above discussion shows, the stakes in terms of exposure, are extremely high. A scenario-development exercise seems appropriate for analyzing such a high-stakes, uncertain issue.

Several different scenarios concerning prospects for the international debt crisis have been posited. In general these scenarios fall into three different camps or schools of thought: the case-by-case recovery, systemic write-down and swap, and debtor cartel perspectives. In the following discussion these contending scenarios about the future of the international debt crisis will be described and then critiqued. Based on this analysis, a recommended strategic response will be given as well.

The case-by-case recovery scenario is essentially one that depicts the current strategy toward the debt crisis as being successful. This strategy can be traced back to how the first rescheduling cases, most notably Zaire, were handled in the 1970s. Although the specifics of each rescheduling agreement may differ in some respects, such as the exact interest rate charged on old and new money, the amount of service fees, and the length of time the debt is rescheduled, all these agreements are guided by certain common principles. These principles included, most fundamentally, the rescheduling of principal payments only; that is, interest payments were kept current and not capitalized. Any new money was paid in proportion to each creditor's existing exposure. Finally, these rescheduling agreements were typically accompanied or preceded by a negotiated stand-by loan program between the country and the International Monetary Fund. Vocal advocates or predictors of this approach or scenario include Paul Volcker, James Baker, Martin Feldstein, Robert Hormats, Jacques de Larosiere, the World Bank, many money center banks, and William Cline. Comparing the projections of Cline and the IMF may be particularly instructive.

Cline presented the first sophisticated and theoretical model in support of the case-by-case approach in mid–1983.[14] The model had a number of assumptions, the most critical being that the marginal elasticity of less developed country (LDC) export volume with regard to growth rates of industrial countries within the Organization of Economic Cooperation and Development (OECD) was three. Thus for each percentage rise in OECD growth, LDC export volume increases by 3 percent. As Cline states,

> Using this model, my estimates in mid–1983 indicated that the debt problem was indeed one of illiquidity rather than insolvency. Under central expectations for international economic variables (and politically acceptable growth rates in debtor countries), the projections showed that most major countries would show substantial improvements in balance of payments and relative debt burden, and that by the late 1980s, debt-export ratio would be back to levels previously associated with creditworthiness. . . . The analysis also indicated that a critical threshold of 2½ to 3 percent was required for OECD growth to avoid stagnation or severe deterioration in external deficits and debt-export ratios for debtor countries.[15]

After two years of managing the debt crisis on a case-by-case basis, Cline declared, "At the end of 1984, it appears that the debtor countries whose debt has systemic consequences are on track for recovery from the debt crisis."[16] Cline's optimism stemmed from the fact that "the centerpiece of debt recovery has materialized: recovery in the international economy."[17] As a result, the eight major Latin American debtor countries increased export earnings by 12 percent in 1984. Based on this experience, Cline predicted the following for the 1985–87 period.

> Projections using updated information through mid–1984 reconfirm the broad analysis that the debt problem is manageable. Even assuming some slowdown in OECD growth (2.7 percent in 1985, 2.3 percent in 1986 and 3 percent in 1987), relatively high interest rates (LIBOR at 12.5 percent in 1984, declining to 9.5 percent only by 1987); and assuming a 20 percent decline of the dollar phased over 1985–86 and oil at $29 per barrel, the ratio of net debt to exports of goods and services declines from 200 percent in 1983 to 140 percent by 1987 for the 19 largest debtor countries. . . . Moreover, these projections provide for debtor-country growth at politically acceptable rates of 4½ percent or more per year. And the projections indicate expansion of nominal export earnings at a faster average rate (14.2 percent, 1984–87) than the level of the interest rate (about 12.5 percent including spread).[18]

Over the next year, however, these projections proved overly optimistic. In 1985 LDC export volume grew more slowly than in the previous year. Even more significant, the dollar value of these exports actually declined from 1984 levels by 6 percentage points.[19] As a result, the IMF commented that "the precarious medium-term prospects for the more highly indebted capital-importing countries underline the need to further develop the efforts that have been underway since 1982 to strengthen the position of these countries.''[20] This precarious position is related mainly to the high vulnerability of debtor countries to external factors, such as the slowdown in OECD growth, continuing weak commodity prices, and persistently high real interest rates in 1985. As Table 33 shows, IMF projections under their baseline scenario indicate rising debt-service payments for debtor countries into the late 1980s (from 36.9 percent in 1985 to 38.1 percent in 1989), even when assuming average annual OECD growth rates of 3 percent. A major factor explaining this trend was the sluggish-to-moderate growth in debtor countries' export volume—1.4 percent in 1985, 0.6 percent in 1986, and an average of a little over 4 percent between 1987 and 1991. Another important factor was related to the inadequate adjustment policies within debtor countries.[21]

Cline and the IMF, therefore, disagree on the relative impact of OECD growth rates on LDC exports.[22] In large part this disagreement stems from their different perspectives on the causes of the international debt crisis. Cline heavily stressed external factors: over half the debt was due to the oil shocks, 20 percent to the 1981–82 recession, and a little under 10 percent to high real interest rates.[23] The IMF, on the other hand, placed far more emphasis on factors internal to the debtor countries. As the IMF stated in April 1986,

> The most frequently cited cause of the deteriorating external debt situation of the capital importing countries was the series of external shocks of 1979–83 that to some extent affected all developing countries. But domestic developments prior to that time, as well as earlier external debt management policies greatly influenced the vulnerability of capital-importing countries to these external shocks.[24]

Eduardo Wiesner, the IMF Director for the Western Hemisphere Department, was even more blunt.

> No other set of factors explains more of the debt crisis than the fiscal deficits incurred by most of the major countries in Latin America. Although there were other factors which were relevant, I have no doubt that the main problem was excessive public (and private) spending. . . . The world recession and high real rates of interest in international markets aggravated the crisis, but I do not believe they created it. What actually happened was that previous domestic macroeconomic policies had made economies more vulnerable to exogenous factors.[25]

Because of actual slippage in the progress of debtor countries in 1985, and based on their own projections, the IMF was from the outset a strong supporter of the Baker plan. In effect their support for the ''U.S. initiative,'' as the IMF likes to call the Baker plan, was an indication that the IMF did not share Cline's optimism. In essence the IMF said that the 1982–85 case-by-case approach could not be continued on ''automatic pilot'' because

Table 33
IMF Baseline Scenario, 1986–1991

	Average 1977-81[1]	1982	1983	1984	1985	1986	1987	Average 1988-91[1]
Industrial countries								
Growth of real GNP	2.7	-0.4	2.6	4.7	2.8	3.0	3.2	3.0
Real six-month LIBOR[2]	3.4	7.1	6.2	7.1	5.3	4.2	4.5	4.2
Increase in GNP deflator	8.4	7.3	4.9	4.3	3.9	3.4	3.0	3.7
World economy								
Change in world price of manufacturers[3]	8.7	-2.5	-3.3	-3.7	1.0	14.0	4.5	4.5
Change in world price of oil[3]	23.6	-4.2	-11.7	-2.1	-4.4	-40.0	-6.3	4.5
Change in world price of non-oil primary commodities[3]	4.6	-10.1	7.1	3.7	-12.2	12.0	1.0	4.2
Growth of total external credit to capital importing countries[3 4]	19.7	13.5	6.2	5.3	5.7	6.2	5.0	5.3
Private	21.4	14.4	3.7	3.6	4.1	4.3	3.3	3.1
Official	16.2	11.6	12.3	9.0	9.1	9.9	8.4	9.0
Capital importing developing countries								
Growth of real GDP	4.9	2.1	1.6	4.7	4.2	3.5	4.2	4.7
Growth of import volume	7.1	-6.5	-2.7	4.6	2.6	2.3	4.2	4.9
Growth of export volume	5.1	-1.5	7.5	10.7	2.5	4.1	5.6	4.8
Countries with recent debt-servicing problems								
Growth of real GDP	4.0	-0.1	-2.5	2.6	2.8	1.9	3.3	4.1
Growth of import volume	5.1	-14.6	-15.0	1.8	-2.7	2.3	2.8	4.8
Growth of export volume	3.3	-4.2	5.4	7.0	1.4	0.6	4.5	4.2

	Average 1977-81	1982	1983	1984	1985	1986	1987	1988	1991
Capital importing developing countries		(As a ratio of exports of goods and services)							
Current account balance	-14.1	-17.8	-9.4	-4.1	-4.9	-6.8	-6.0	-5.8	-5.9
Total external debt	122.6	148.6	158.8	152.8	163.0	166.6	160.7	150.0	140.2
Debt service payments	18.4	23.6	22.0	22.9	24.1	24.2	22.6	23.7	21.7
Interest payments	8.1	13.6	13.0	13.1	13.2	13.0	12.1	11.3	10.3
Amortization payments	10.3	10.1	9.1	9.8	10.9	11.3	10.5	12.5	11.4
Countries with recent debt-servicing problems									
Current account balance	-20.6	-29.9	-10.2	-3.9	-2.2	-6.8	-4.6	-3.6	-2.4
Total external debt	166.8	234.5	252.3	244.2	260.6	275.4	261.0	232.7	206.4
Debt service payments	27.4	38.2	34.4	35.1	36.9	37.7	34.8	38.1	31.9
Interest payments	11.9	23.3	22.4	22.6	23.0	23.0	21.0	19.3	16.9
Amortization payments	15.5	14.9	12.0	12.5	13.8	14.7	13.8	18.8	15.0

[1]Compound annual rates of change.
[2]London interbank offered rate on six-month U.S. dollar deposits, deflated by the U.S. GNP deflator.
[3]In U.S. dollars.
[4]Includes trade financing.

Source: IMF, World Economic Outlook, April 1986, p 92.

> for many heavily indebted countries . . . the adjustment that has occurred has yet to yield a favorable growth performance. It is this weak performance that has led to a set of proposals put forth by the United States Secretary of the Treasury.[26]

The Baker plan, announced at the annual meeting of the World Bank and the Fund at Seoul, South Korea, in October 1985, had three major features. According to U.S. Treasury Secretary, James Baker, the "first and foremost" feature was "the adoption by principal debtor countries of comprehensive macroeconomic and structural policies, supported by the international financial institutions, to promote growth and balance-of-payments adjustments, and to reduce inflation."[27] These reform policies included privatizing state-owned enterprises, reducing government budget deficits, implementing tax cuts and supply-side incentives, liberalizing trade, and promoting foreign direct investment. Such policies, in all likelihood, would discourage or reverse the massive capital outflows from debtor countries, estimated at nearly $31 billion from the ten major Latin American debtors in 1983–85.[28] Solving the capital flight problem was critical to the Baker plan.

> As a practical matter, it is unrealistic to call upon the support of voluntary lending from abroad, whether public or private, when domestic funds are moving in the other direction. Capital flight must be reversed if there is to be any real prospect of additional funding, whether debt or equity. If a country's own citizens have no confidence in its economic system, how can others?[29]

To support and direct these reform policies, Baker saw as his plan's second major feature: "a continued central role for the IMF, in conjunction with increased and more effective structural adjustment lending by the multilateral development banks, both in support of the adoption by principal debtors of market-oriented policies for growth."[30] Besides the IMF continuing its central role, the Fund and the World Bank would be encouraged to increase their collaboration. The World Bank, moreover, was asked to play a larger, more important role in the debt crisis. In particular the Bank's policy-based lending, which began in 1980 with the start of Structural Adjustment Loans (SALs), would be considerably enhanced. In fact the Bank was expected to increase non-project lending to 20 percent of total credits, from the current level of 11 percent.[31]

The third feature of the plan outlined by Baker was "increased lending by the private banks in support of comprehensive economic adjustment programs."[32] This new lending would equal $20 billion and would be extended to fifteen targeted countries over three years. (See Table 34.) Such financing would amount to an increase in U.S. banks' total exposure to Latin America of between 2 and 3 percent a year. New money from official sources—the IMF, World Bank, and other multilateral agencies—would total approximately $20 billion over the same three years.

Table 34
Fifteen Targeted Debtors in the Baker Plan

	Total External Debt			1985 Interest Payments			
Country	in Billions	%GNP	% Exports	in Billions	%GNP	%Exports	Debt Service Ratio
Brazil	$103.5	51	368	$11.8	5.8	41	41
Mexico	97.7	62	322	10.0	6.3	33	59
Argentina	50.8	79	483	5.1	7.9	52	80
Venezuela	32.6	64	201	4.1	8.1	18	34
Philippines	27.4	81	342	2.1	6.2	28	35
Chile	21.9	135	442	2.1	12.9	43	53
Yugoslavia	20.0	42	160	1.7	3.6	15	26
Nigeria	18.0	19	180	1.8	1.9	13	40
Morocco	14.4	118	430	1.0	8.2	26	48
Peru	13.9	116	370	1.3	10.8	31	33
Colombia	13.9	35	259	1.3	3.3	34	22
Ecuador	7.9	68	254	0.7	6.0	24	34
Ivory Coast	6.3	91	212	0.6	8.7	18	18
Uruguay	4.9	96	395	0.5	9.8	36	45
Bolivia	4.2	105	453	0.4	10.0	8	22
Total	437.4	77	324	44.5	7.3	28	39

Source: Morgan Guaranty, *World Financial Markets*, September/October 1985, p. 4; *Fortune*, December 25, 1985, p. 101; and *Economist*, January 11, 1986, p. 71.

The Baker plan was essentially a continuation of the case-by-case approach, albeit in a more intensified and comprehensive form. The evolving circumstances of 1985 had made a major new initiative seem necessary. Besides adverse macroeconomic trends for nearly all major debtors, particularly in export performance, the case of Mexico was especially disturbing. Having been depicted as the model of the case-by-case approach, which rewarded the country with the first multiyear rescheduling pact, Mexico fell on hard times in 1985. Signs of trouble emerged as early as January, even before the new debt agreement was officially signed in April. Most disturbing, the rate of inflation surged by 7.4 percent in that month alone, partially caused by the monetizing of a higher fiscal deficit than allowed under the IMF program. Renewed capital flight also accelerated the devaluation of the peso, which became even more overvalued in light of government controls. That is, these devaluations did not keep pace with relative inflation rates between the United States and Mexico. Of course, softening oil prices greatly exacerbated this deteriorating economic situation. By early September, the Mexican government felt compelled to declare its displeasure with current debt agreements and the overall approach to the problem being followed by the IMF and OECD countries. For the first time, a high-ranking Mexican government official, Finance Minister Silva Herzog, publicly voiced sympathy for measures that would link debt payments to export earnings and the capitalization of interest payments. President de la Madrid, in fact, simultaneously reinforced Herzog by publicly insisting that unless a "new formula" was found, a renewed debt crisis would ensue.[33] A few days after these comments were made, a massive earthquake hit Mexico City. It was now obvious to nearly everyone that a different approach to the debt crisis was vital. Mexico, in this sense, was the catalyst behind the Baker plan. Mexico, in fact, was prominently designated by U.S. officials as the most likely candidate for launching the Baker initiative when it was announced in October 1985.

It should be stressed, however, that the advocates of the Baker plan do not consider the initiative to have been born out of the failure of the earlier case-by-case approach. Instead the Baker plan was seen as the logical extension of crisis-management measures that largely succeeded in the 1982–84 period. As Martin Feldstein said more than a year before the plan was announced, "Although the current strategy has been successful in dealing with the initial stage of the financial crisis, the time has come to shift from crisis management to a policy of promoting Latin American growth."[34] Two years later, the IMF echoed these comments:

> The debt-servicing difficulties that came to a head in 1982 were handled with a considerable degree of success by strong measures and cooperative efforts of debtor country governments, creditor institutions (and their respective monetary authorities) and the Fund. Nevertheless . . . problems remain. . . . The disappointing growth performance of a number of countries has been due both to relative weakness of the recovery in the industrial world, and to the fact that many indebted countries

> have given insufficient emphasis to the adjustments needed to stimulate the growth of domestic productive capacity. . . . At the same time, the greater emphasis on growth-oriented adjustment programs, urged in the U.S. initiative, strengthens the efforts of the Fund in promoting policies conducive to economic growth.[35]

Thus, the Baker plan was seen by the Fund to be a strengthening of a successful case-by-case approach.

Alternatively, the so-called Bradley plan envisions a different scenario or resolution of the international debt crisis. As spelled out by U.S. Senator Bill Bradley in the summer of 1986, the plan is based on three principles.

> First, we have to make clear to Latin America that our objective is a partnership of growth. The idea has to be to address the fundamental problems of poverty and malnutrition that exist there. Second, our proposal has to be seen as bold enough to be a cure, not a palliative, not a marginal assist. And third, we have to say to them, "We will help, but what are you willing to do?" Instead of telling them, "You must do the following before you get help." A shift of emphasis like that makes all the difference in the world in Latin America.[36]

For Bradley, a partnership in growth, which could be seen in Latin America as a bold offer of help, required a debt write-down on the part of commercial banks. Specifically, Bradley proposed measures that would relieve two-thirds of Latin American debtors' annual $30 billion debt burden. These measures included a reduction in the interest rate of three percentage points over a three-year period, forgiving 3 percent of the loan principal over the same time period, and $3 billion a year from the World Bank and other multilateral institutions. The exact percentages and loan volume, however, were negotiable, for as Bradley stated, "the precise numbers aren't all that important, but the concept of debt relief is."[37] These arrangements would be negotiated at an international conference, called the "Trade Debt Summit." The summit would meet in conjunction with the multilateral discussions on trade, held under the aegis of the General Agreement on Tariffs and Trade (GATT). Such a linkage between trade and debt negotiations would reflect the importance of this relationship in resolving the debt crisis.

Bradley saw his proposals as a replacement for the Baker plan. In fact Bradley declared that "the highly touted Baker debt initiative is a failure."[38] Clearly, Bradley was glad to make the declaration because from his perspective the Baker plan was seriously flawed in a number of respects. First, the tone of the Baker approach made it politically difficult, if not impossible, for debtor countries to adopt. Second, the Baker initiative failed to directly address net capital outflows from debtor countries. For example, around $40 billion in new lending was proposed by Baker for a three-year period, but the annual interest payments of the fifteen targeted countries approached $45 billion. Third, the Baker plan called for more commercial bank exposure at a time when the external debt obligations of these countries was already too high: "In other words, the Baker plan prolongs the policies that created the debt crisis in the first place."[39]

The Bradley proposals have a great deal of support from academics and practioners alike. Proponents of a systematic write-down of the debt, facilitated by international agreements and organizations, include Felix Rohatyn, several business periodicals and consulting services, Helmut Schmidt, the Overseas Development Council, the Inter-American Dialogue Group, and the highly respected economist Rudiger Dornbusch.[40] Given the running debate between Dornbusch and Cline over the last few years, a close look at Dornbusch's arguments is particularly appropriate. A comparison of Cline and Dornbusch, moreover, will provide the intellectual underpinnings of these two contending scenarios.

Dornbusch, like Cline, agrees that "OECD growth is invariably the central figure of any assessment of the future of the debt crisis."[41] Unlike Cline, however, Dornbusch argues that the exact "elasticity estimate of LDC export growth with respect to OECD growth cannot be pinned down."[42] Thus the Cline link of 3:1 is challenged on the basis of data bias, in that Cline's regression analysis used data on total OECD import growth. Given that non-oil LDCs export accounts for only 17 percent of total OECD imports, Cline's estimates are questioned. Attempts by Dornbusch to measure the exact impact of OECD growth on non-oil LDC exports produces uncertain results: "The instability of the estimates is so large that these high estimates are to a large extent an artifact of the 1974–76 period."[43]

With these differences in mind, Dornbusch assumes the "first-best" macroeconomic scenario, which would mean "a transitory European fiscal expansion, a long-term fiscal tightening in the United States and an accommodating monetary policy."[44] Such a scenario would cause moderate OECD growth, lower or stable real interest rates, and a dollar decline. Dornbusch, moreover, sees this set of outcomes as the most likely scenario:

> [The] outlook makes it clear that neither dollar collapse nor high sustained growth can be expected. Nor, on the other hand, should one expect protracted recession or sharp increases in interest rates. In sum the scenario for OECD countries provides a neutral setting for any LDC that does not, as yet, have debt difficulties. Problem debtors should not expect rapid relief. For Latin debtors, most of the relief must come from their domestic adjustment or a rewriting of the debt.[45]

Dornbusch, therefore, reaches macroeconomic conclusions which are similar to the IMF's baseline scenario in the 1986 *World Economic Outlook*. As was shown in Table 33, the IMF's baseline scenario forecasts around 3 percent annual OECD growth for 1986–91, a slow drop in the dollar of 2.5 percent per year, and slightly declining and stable real interest rates. Dornbusch and the IMF also agree on a more uncertain and perhaps lower elasticity estimate for LDC exports with respect to OECD growth. The IMF and Dornbusch disagree, however, concerning the proper response to this scenario and set of assumptions. Of the two options of solving the debt crisis—emphasizing LDC domestic adjustment or by rewriting the debt—the IMF clearly favors the former option and Dornbusch, the latter. As Dornbusch states,

> U.S. policy in the debt question has favored the muddling-through strategy of rescheduling loans short-term at considerable spreads. . . . Muddling through is poor policy because it does not, in the near term, return the debtor economics to reasonably functioning market economies, poorer but with employment and hope. Muddling through has, for all intents and purposes, created siege economics. The only constructive alternative I see is to work on a double front: in the developed countries, import barriers must be removed and banks must write down some debts (of interest and principal) in exchange for stabilization programs that have as performance criteria not budget cuts but real exchange rates and export growth.[46]

A focal point of Dornbusch's concern is clearly on the political stability of debtor countries. Dornbusch, in fact, sees LDCs as having reached "debt service fatigue," perhaps being no longer able or willing to continue painful austerity programs.[47] Bradley agrees: "If we fail to establish a partnership for growth with the present set of democratic leaders in Latin America, I can imagine repercussions that will put another set of people in power who share neither our commitment to the present international financial system or to the market system."[48]

In essence the divergence between the case-by-case recovery and systemic write-down scenarios, as espoused by Baker and the IMF versus Dornbusch and Bradley, is rooted in questions of political risk and instability. The recommended response of governments and international organizations thus differs because of these contending risk perceptions. For Baker, the IMF, and other case-by-case advocates, creditor governments and international organizations should continue to facilitate the consummation of freely negotiated rescheduling agreements and then monitor their implementation. For Bradley, Dornbusch, and other systemic write-down advocates, creditor governments and international organizations must act more forceably to prevent a political crisis. By implication, government bodies should dictate a write-down of the debt. The extent of the write-down would perhaps vary by country and would be determined via government-dominated negotiations at the debt summit *cum* GATT meetings.

The worst political risk scenario for the international banking community, of course, concerns a third possible outcome for the debt crisis—unilateral LDC action, perhaps in the form of a debtor cartel. The best known and most vocal of the debtor-cartel proponents, Fidel Castro, promotes the view that the debt crisis could cause massive political instability in Latin America. As Castro recently observed,

> The political, economic and social situation of Latin America is such that it can't hold up under any more restrictions and sacrifices. . . . If a solution isn't found for

> the economic crisis—and above all for the crisis of the debt—South America is going to explode.[49]

Castro advocates that debtor countries "cut out the cancer of debt" via repudiations.[50] This approach to the debt crisis was loudly pronounced at the debt conference in Havana, held mainly for Latin American trade union leaders in July 1985.

Debt repudiations could be made jointly by LDCs in a debtors' cartel or by individual countries acting alone. The most likely organization from which a debtors' cartel could spring is the Cartagena group, formed in June 1983 by eleven debtor countries. By the summer of 1984, a coordinated strategy aiming for interest rate caps and ceilings on debt-service payments became the focal point of discussion within the Cartagena group. These topics received renewed attention in July 1985 when Mexico called and held a secret meeting of the Cartagena group, minus Argentina, at Oaxtapec. Subsequently, Mexican officials have insisted upon interest rate relief or caps and debt-service payments tied to oil prices for export earnings in their negotiations with commercial banks, the IMF, and the United States during the spring and summer of 1986. So far there have been no formal joint declarations by the Cartagena group or any other set of debtor countries that unilaterally implements such measures.[51]

At the individual country level, however, such unilateral declarations have been made, most notably in Peru by President Alan Garcia. When inaugurated in July 1985, Garcia declared that Peru would limit debt-service payments to 10 percent of export earnings and that official lenders would be paid before commercial banks. In September 1985 Peru made an almost unprecedented move by missing a payment to the IMF. Garcia even barred the IMF from sending a negotiating team to Peru. By October 1985, U.S. regulators declared Peruvian loans as "value-impaired," thus forcing commercial banks to set aside reserves to cover a potential write-off. Although the country was technically in default, banks have chosen not to make that declaration, hoping that Peru, like Bolivia, will reverse its path toward economic autarchy and fearing that too harsh a reaction against Peru might make Garcia a martyr to be emulated by other debtor countries. The U.S. government apparently agrees with this approach, for the Baker plan included Peru in its target list, in effect saying, "Come home and all will be forgiven."[52]

Determining the relative probability of the Castro-Garcia approach to the debt crisis as opposed to the Baker or Bradley plans requires extensive analysis. Most critically, the key drivers that will impact the debt crisis need to be identified. Various driver outcomes and their likelihood of occurring must also be posited, necessitating an explicit statement of underlying assumptions as well. The most likely driver outcomes, if internally consistent, can then be combined to form the most likely scenario. At that point, reasonable probability estimates can be made.

According to nearly all accounts, the single most important driver impacting prospects for the international debt crisis is OECD growth rates.[53] For example, Cline's model says that a change of one percentage point in the growth of industrialized countries has four times the effect of a 10 percent change in the value of the U.S. dollar and five times the impact of a one-percentage-point change in the interest rate. Possible driver outcomes over a five-year period include high and sustained OECD growth of well above 3 percent a year, moderate and cyclical growth of around 3 percent annually, and stagnant, recessionary growth of well under 3 percent a year. Interestingly, economists representing different schools of thought, or radically different positions toward the debt crisis, reach similar conclusions about probable OECD growth and its impact on debtor countries. Both the IMF and Dornbusch forecast moderate OECD growth rates averaging around 3 percent annually for 1986–91.

These forecasts, moreover, seem quite reasonable and the most likely to develop. If one looks at past average growth rates in industrialized countries, a 3 percent growth rate is a mid-range forecast. Whereas the 1960s exhibited 4–5 percent growth, the 1970s and early 1980s averaged a little over 3 and 2 percent respectively.[54] However, in view of the slow rate of 1985 OECD growth of well under 3 percent and the general sluggishness of the world economy since 1979, further stagnation and recessionary growth is possible, especially if the U.S. dollar's value rapidly declines as the U.S. federal budget deficit remains large. This outcome would mean the collapse of the bond market, rising real interest rates, and a severe recession.[55] The moderate growth-rate forecast, therefore, assumes a gradual and steady reduction in the U.S. fiscal deficit as a percentage of GNP and a fairly stable exchange rate for the U.S. dollar. Conversely, a high and sustained OECD growth rate, the least likely driver outcome, would have to assume not only a steady U.S. fiscal deficit reduction, but fiscal stimulus in other OECD countries, most notably Japan and Germany, and a major tax reform stimulus to the U.S. economy as well.

Another critical development that would preclude a high and sustained level of OECD growth would be a dramatic and rapid increase in oil prices to well over $20 per barrel, which could constitute a third oil shock to the global economy. In fact the importance of oil prices in determining outcomes for the debt crisis is so high as to warrant it being a driver. Certainly, the first and second oil shocks were key in causing the debt crisis, when the first led to petrodollar recycling and the massive LDC debt and the second to the inability of many debtors to meet their credit obligations. The future of oil prices is just as tied to political decisions within and around certain countries as it is to economic factors such as OECD growth rates. Thus oil prices should be a key driver in any scenario development exercise about the debt crisis because it is a significant, direct, and autonomous force in this issue.

Interestingly, the impact of oil prices on the debt crisis is perhaps the opposite of what most people expect, that is, falling oil prices hurt debtors more than rising prices. Both the Cline and IMF models show this relationship, which is due to the fact that "major debtors as a group are oil exporters on balance" and "the value of net exports by developing to industrial countries increases when oil prices go up."[56] Such a viewpoint, however, is misleading, for it suffers from the blindness of aggregation; namely, the impact of oil prices on all debtors, determined by macroeconomic and balance-of-payment averages, may obscure an important point or fact about the debt crisis. A select few countries, because of their size (in terms of total debt exposure, GNP, and geopolitical importance), may be bellwether cases that will shape or determine the outcome of the debt crisis. As President de la Madrid stated, "Where the debt is concerned, the domino theory must be kept in mind. If a heavy piece falls, the whole game can collapse."[57] Smaller countries, on the other hand, can be isolated and prevented from having any major, systemic impact on the international debt crisis. Bolivia, for example, in stopping debt payments, was contained for two years until inevitable economic hardships forced the country to reverse course and rejoin the international financial community. The same fate may be in store for Peru. It is doubtful that such small countries with limited internal resources can practice quasi-economic autarchy for very long.

From this perspective, it matters little if oil prices rapidly and dramatically rise or fall. Since the big dominos include Brazil, Argentina, and Mexico, which comprise nearly 60 percent of the total external debt of the Baker targets, any kind of oil shock will severely affect at least one of these major players in the debt crisis. In this sense the best-case outcome for oil prices in the 1986–91 period would be for a gradual rise to around $20 per barrel by 1991. Such a rise would aid a distressed Mexico, which was severely hurt by the rapid oil price decline of 1985–86, and would not be overly stressful to the Brazilian economy.

This best-case outcome, by a small margin, is the most likely for the 1986–91 period. Oil prices, which plunged to around $10 a barrel on the spot market in 1986, were driven to that low depth by fundamental global supply and demand factors; there was also a political decision in Saudi Arabia to overproduce and help glut the world market. All these factors, however, will not have a lasting impact. Well before 1991, global crude supply will decrease when most marginal producers are driven out by low prices and when Saudi Arabia subsequently decides to cut back on the oil flow from their vast petroleum reserves. At the same time, world demand for oil will have grown as some old consumption habits return with low prices and as OECD growth rates average around 3 percent a year.

A dramatic and rapid increase in the price of oil to the $25–$30 per barrel level by or before 1991 is relatively unlikely. Institutionalized conservation measures, more alternative forms of energy, and strategic petroleum reserves are in place in most OECD countries, and OPEC is no longer dominant in the world oil market. In other words the special circumstances of 1973–74 are not present. An outcome of rapidly rising oil prices in the next five years, therefore, seems dependent on political factors, primarily war or revolution. The Iran-Iraq war spilling over into the Arab, Persian Gulf states or revolution in Saudi Arabia are two possibilities.

A third key driver concerns real interest rates, which directly affect debtor countries since over half their debt is tied to either LIBOR or U.S. interest rates. For Mexico, for example, a one percentage drop in the interest rates saves the country $800 million a year in debt-service payments. Although real interest rates are related to GNP trends, many other factors influence their rise or fall, such as inflation, monetary and fiscal policy, and exchange rate developments.

The best-case outcome for real interest rates would be their continued and significant decline. Preconditions for such a trend include continued low inflation and monetary restraint, a dramatic decline in the U.S. fiscal deficit as a percentage of GNP, and fairly stable foreign exchange rates. Certainly, real rates of interest, although declining significantly in the first half of 1986, remain at historically high levels, leaving room for further drops.

It is unlikely, however, that all of these preconditions will be present, particularly a dramatic decline in the U.S. fiscal deficit as a percentage of GNP. First, it is not clear that a quick and drastic reduction in the deficit is wise, given its possible recessionary impact on the U.S. economy. Second, reducing the fiscal deficit to a level of 2 percent of GNP from the current 5.5 percent is expecting too much given the hard political choices and pressures facing the U.S. government. A slightly higher level of U.S. inflation is also probable, given dollar devaluation, oil price trends, growth rates, and a loosening of monetary restraints at the U.S. Federal Reserve Board (Fed.). These restraints will be loosened because supply-siders will be more influential at the Fed. in the post–Volcker era. Thus real interest rates may come down by a slight amount, but not much. This most probable outcome echoes IMF forecasts.[58] The possibility, of course, exists for rising real interest rates if inflation gets out of control or if the U.S. dollar plummets in a high fiscal-deficit environment. The September 1985 agreement at the New York Plaza Hotel by the Group of Five and the resulting managed decline of the dollar, however, makes this worst-case outcome much more unlikely.

The last driver to be considered concerns the international trade environment. Obviously, even if there is high OECD growth, it matters little to LDCs if their goods are increasingly shut out of industrial country markets. All economic projections would be off if OECD protectionism dramatically increases. Indeed, since the debt crisis started trade complaints and barriers against debtor-country exports have risen but not yet to crisis proportions.

This worst-case outcome for trade is unlikely to develop for a number of reasons. Perhaps most importantly, the international procedures and organizations in support of trade liberalization are extremely strong and widespread. Such support is strengthened by the collective experience of the 1930s. Significant increases in trade protectionism are usually associated with major economic recessions, and if most forecasts about OECD growth rates are correct, such an economic slump will be avoided. Lastly, the main stimulus behind protectionist bills, the large U.S. trade deficit, should moderate during 1987, given the fall of the U.S. dollar that has occurred in 1985–86.

The present global political and economic environment also makes it relatively unlikely for major reductions in trade barriers through international negotiations. Unemployment rates in OECD countries remain too high, and it is politically difficult, if not impossible, for governments to implement the major kinds of structural adjustments that significantly lower trade barriers would require. The most likely outcome, therefore, for the international trade environment over the next few years is for the status quo to continue, with perhaps additional orderly marketing agreements (OMAs) being negotiated. As with exchange rates, attempts are being made to manage trade relations multilaterally. At present, a basic and increasingly important tool in such management is the negotiation of market share agreements or OMAs. In this way governments reach acceptable economic and political compromises that maintain, although in suboptimal form, a liberalized trade environment. This approach to the management of trade disputes has been in place for at least two decades and will probably continue into the foreseeable future.

Combining the most likely driver outcomes, therefore, leads to a scenario of moderate OECD growth, gradually rising oil prices, slightly lower and stable real rates of interest, and a continued overall liberal trade environment, albeit with more OMAs. These outcomes are internally consistent and plausible. Of the three contending schools of thought regarding how the debt crisis should be managed, the case-by-case approach, epitomized at present by the Baker plan, clearly fits this scenario the best. These driver outcomes help debtor countries. The probable success of the Baker plan rises as external environmental conditions for LDCs improve.

Even so, for the Baker plan to work, more debt relief than formally and initially offered is required because of obvious cash flow problems associated with the U.S. initiative. A serious flaw in the plan is that only around $40 billion in new money over three years flows into the fifteen LDCs, as opposed to $45 billion per year in interest payments going out of the targeted debtor countries. How can these countries grow, a primary objective of the Baker plan, if such capital-scarce debtors suffer net capital outflows?

The Baker-Volcker-Larosiere team may have the answers to this cash-flow problem. One obvious answer is flexibility, which would allow new lending at a much higher level than originally intended. The Mexican rescue package of 1986 involves over $12 billion in new money for the remainder of 1986 and 1987 and if implemented would strongly signal such flexibility. A second answer may involve an increase in debt for equity swaps, which would reduce the debt burden of developing countries. Significantly, bank regulators have ruled that such swaps, when debt is traded at a discount for equity position in foreign companies, do not result in other loans to the country being classified as value-impaired. Consequently, the volume of such swaps has accelerated and now totals $3 billion for five major debtors: the Philippines, Chile, Brazil, Mexico, and Argentina. Unfortunately, this total is small compared to their total debt of $220 billion, and projections estimate that the potential for swaps in these countries will rise to $5 billion a year if their investment climates improve. At best, therefore, debt for equity swaps are only partial solutions to the cash-flow problems of debtor countries.

As a result, there may be a third answer to this problem, and it may be rooted in a possible secret agenda of the Baker plan, namely interest-payment relief. Volcker is known to be sympathetic toward interest rate caps, but he feels that the timing of their implementation is crucial. Interest rate caps before a Baker plan is in place would reduce the incentive not only for banks to lend new money but for debtor countries to implement needed structural adjustment policies. In any event interest rate caps above present rates do not solve the cash-flow problem. Perhaps by necessity, real debt relief requires the capitalization and long-term rescheduling of interest payments and/or big reductions in the rate of interest on current and future debt.

The case of Mexico in 1986–87 might illustrate how the Baker plan might be made to work. In July 1986 an IMF agreement with Mexico was signed, the first attempt to implement the U.S. initiative. The agreement is unique for the IMF in that growth, not austerity, is the goal. Future bank lending will be tied to Mexican growth rates and international oil prices. In exchange Mexico promises to implement fundamental structural reforms. As shown in Chapter 3, Mexico seems to have a stable enough political base to make the implementation of these reforms possible (see Table 13).

Of the $12 billion in new money that will go to Mexico in 1986–87, half the amount will take the form of new commercial bank loans. By October 1986, these new loans were agreed to in principle by the thirteen-bank steering committee that negotiates Mexican rescheduling agreements for the nearly five hundred commercial banks with exposure in the country. The terms of the commercial bank agreement with Mexico are listed in Table 35.

The agreement is significant in a number of respects: it is a move toward real long-term rescheduling of debt; interest rates are lowered from the 1⅛ above LIBOR level of the 1984–85 agreement; the World Bank for the first time is guaranteeing a portion of the new commercial bank debt; and the principle of automatic contingency funding is now in place. From a cash-flow perspective, the agreement addresses many of Mexico's needs. The amount of new money is substantial, and Mexico will not be burdened formally with any principal payments for several years. Mexico's annual interest bill will be reduced by $500 million for each of the next ten years, given current rates of interest and the differential between the 13/16 and 1⅛ margins.

The total interest bill for 1986–87, however, will still exceed the $12 billion in new money by about $1 billion. This is an improvement over the tremendous net outflow of funds in previous years. The above comparison between total interest payments and new money ignores the fact that Mexico has already paid

Table 35
Commercial Bank–Mexican Rescheduling Agreement, October 1986

	Issue	Agreement in Principle
I.	Basic Terms	
	1. Restructured Debt = $43.7 billion	7 years grace on principal payments 20 years final maturity 13/16 above Libor margin
	2. Old, new money = $8.8 billion loaned after 1982	Repaid in 1989-94 in equal installments 13/16 above Libor margin
	3. New, new money = $6.0 billion to be loaned in 1986-87	5 year grace period 12 years final maturity 13/16 above Libor margin

II. Basic Principles

1. Of the $6 billion in new, new money, $1 billion will be cofinanced with the World Bank
2. Of the $1 billion that is cofinanced with the World Bank, $500 million is guaranteed by the World Bank
3. Contingency Facilities
   a. IMF Oil Contingency = SDR 600 million
   b. Commerical Bank Growth Contingency Cofinancing = $500 million, of which $250 million is guaranteed by the World Bank
   c. Commerical Bank Contingent Investment Support Facility = $1.2 billion to support public and private sector investment.

its interest bill for the first half of 1986, totaling around $4 billion, which means that there is a real net inflow of funds for the remainder of 1986–87. If Mexico's growth does not reach 3 to 4 percent by early 1987, $500 million of contingency money will be automatically released, a likely possibility. A further $1.8 billion in contingency funds will be forthcoming if oil prices drop below $9 a barrel or if Mexico's budget receipts—of which oil accounts for nearly 30 percent—fall so low as to impair the IMF's investment targets for the country. In effect the IMF-engineered plan for Mexico is designed to insure that the country has a net inflow of funds from which it can invest and grow. Thus the international financial community had indicated a willingness to lend enough funds to cover future contingencies and hope that at some point Mexico's ability to generate its own foreign exchange will exceed the accumulation of new debt.

The assumptions behind this plan are varied, but most importantly they include the following. First, the oil price will not plunge further, nor will the pace of Mexican manufactured exports. Second, interest rates will not rise. These assumptions seem reasonable given the earlier macroeconomic and political forecast.

Third and perhaps most critical, capital flight for 1986–87 will be far below previous years. In 1986, for example, the IMF is forecasting capital flight for Mexico at only $800 million, down from $2.5 billion in 1985. This is a critical assumption because of the volatility of this variable and the magnitude of such capital movement in the past, which some estimates say exceeded $16 billion in 1983–85.[59] In fact it is thought that as much as $50 billion of capital flight money is located outside the country. Thus the $800 million dollar figure assumes a slowdown in the rate of capital flight because of renewed confidence in the Mexican political economy as a result of the IMF program and because of working capital requirements in the Mexican private sector. Of course, if capital flight returns to the average of the 1983–85 period, $5.4 billion, Mexican reserves will not increase, a politically important development since the government did not deliver on the promise of interest payment relief, and there would not be a surplus of funds from which Mexico could grow.

The Mexican-IMF agreement of 1986 can also be assessed in terms of the conceptual framework of political economy. It is clear that Mexico's political economy is in "major disequilibrium." An economic performance crisis exists because of the difficulties in repaying the external debt since 1982 and because of the external shock of rapidly falling oil prices in the first half of 1986. This recent external shock has compounded the debt crisis by dramatically reducing export earnings and increasing the fiscal deficit to over 20 percent of Mexico's GNP. The $12 billion loan package is obviously designed to help Mexico overcome these debt repayment and external shock problems.

In fully analyzing the Mexican-IMF agreement of 1986, one should take a future-oriented perspective. A five-year forecast would seem appropriate, and the conceptual framework of political economy can again be helpful in this respect. Throughout the 1987–91 period Mexico will undoubtedly remain in "major disequilibrium" because the debt crisis will not be resolved in those years. The other aspects of the situation should improve, and in fact, indications of progress are already evident. Most importantly, a strategic shift in the country's goals is taking place away from the import-substitution approach of the past and toward a strategy of growth that is based more on export promotion. Signs of this strategic shift are symbolized in four areas: the dramatic speed in trade liberalization through the reduction of import controls; the watershed decision in 1986 to apply for GATT membership; the move toward a relatively uncontrolled peso foreign exchange rate; and the 1985 approval by Mexico of the IBM proposal to form a 100 percent subsidiary in Guadalajara as an export base for their personal computer business. An export-oriented strategy fits the Mexican context fairly well. External markets are secure in that 70 percent of Mexico's trade is with the United States, and no significant increase in trade barriers to that market is likely. Generating foreign exchange earnings through exports is crucial for most countries with heavy debt burdens, and this is certainly the case for Mexico.

The major contextual problem for such a strategic shift in Mexico is the political difficulty of sustaining its implementation. Strong bureaucratic opposition within the government, state-owned enterprises, and the ruling party (the PRI) exists. President de la Madrid, however, has made impressive progress toward reorienting the country's strategy in light of these political obstacles. In other words the management of economic policy has been basically sound, but potential problems loom on the horizon, particularly in light of the strong opposition voiced against the commercial bank agreement with Mexico announced in October 1986 and Mexico's upcoming presidential elections in July 1988. Future IMF and commercial bank agreements with Mexico that will follow the 1986–87 accord must consider the political impact within the country very closely.

Fortunately, one can confidently forecast no major external or internal shocks for Mexico in the 1986–91 period. According to the most likely macroeconomic scenario previously discussed, oil prices are likely to rise gradually, not fall precipitously. A dramatic increase in interest rates is also not likely, and Mexico's political instability potential remains relatively low.

Thus, Mexico is predicted to remain in "major disequilibrium" solely because the huge debt burden will take years to resolve, whereas the other strategic fundamentals look sound: no external or internal shock is expected; the newly emerging country strategy largely fits the context and is starting to have positive economic performance results; and the management of economic policy is impressive given certain political constraints. It will be the responsibility of the international financial community to aid those Mexican officials who want to further the strategic shift to export promotion by structuring future agreements in a way that strengthens the political position of such leaders. Such aid-rendering agreements include the following features: continued emphasis on Mexico's growth, not austerity; additional new money and World Bank guarantees; an even longer-term rescheduling of the debt that goes well beyond twenty years; and most significantly, substantial interest-payment relief.

Such a successful plan for Mexico, or for any one of the Brazil-Argentina-Mexico (BAM) trio, would be critical and could lead to a positive domino effect on other debtor countries. The IMF-Mexican agreement of 1986, however, is burdened by many uncertainties and may eventually require more substantial interest-payment relief for it to work in the long run. Such relief, of course, could have a major adverse impact on the profit and loss statements of major commercial banks, considering their exposure in major debtor countries, as Table 36 indicates. Nevertheless, such a development and sacrifice may be necessary.

In any event the development of the most likely global macroeconomic and political scenario—moderate OECD growth, gradually rising oil prices, lower interest rates, and no major increases in trade barriers—will facilitate the process launched by the IMF-Mexican agreement of 1986. Certainly, this agreement increases the probability that the Baker plan will succeed. Even Senator Bradley admitted as much by saying,

> This could be a step in the right direction, depending on how the banks respond. My sense is that they [the Mexicans] are anticipating some interest-rate relief, and

Table 36
Top Twelve U.S. Banks' Exposures in Top Three Debtor Countries, 1985

Banks	Capitals	Pretax Earnings	Brazil	Mexico	Argentina
Citicorp	7.8(1)	1.72(1)	4.7	2.8	1.4
Bank America Corp.	4.5(4)	-0.43(-)	2.8	2.7	N.A.
Chase Manhattan Corp.	4.5(6)	0.90(7)	2.8	1.7	0.9
J.P. Morgan	4.4(7)	0.92(6)	1.9	1.2	0.8
Manufacturers Hanover Corp.	3.5(11)	0.60(14)	2.2	1.8	1.4
Chemical NY Corp.	2.8(20)	0.53(15)	1.4	1.5	N.A.
First Interstate Bancorp	2.5(27)	0.38(37)	0.5	0.7	N.A.
Bankers Trust NY Corp.	2.5(28)	0.49(24)	0.9	1.3	N.A.
Security Pacific Corp.	2.4(31)	0.50(22)	0.6	0.5	N.A.
First Chicago Corp.	2.1(36)	0.19(79)	0.8	0.9	N.A.
Mellon Bank Corp.	1.6(48)	0.25(61)	0.5	0.6	N.A.
Wells Fargo & Co.	1.5(58)	0.30(50)	0.6	0.6	N.A.
TOTAL	40.1	5.35	19.7	16.3	4.5

- All values in billions of U.S. Dollars
- Figure in parentheses indicate world ranking
- N.A. indicates none or less than 1% exposure of capital

Sources: Various annual reports, 1985.

> that the administration is finally coming to understand that we have a strategic opportunity here in trying to help Mexico restore growth.[60]

In short, the probability of a scenario that shows the case-by-case approach as being successful is estimated subjectively here to be approximately 50 percent.

Both scenarios encapsulated by the Dornbusch-Bradley plans or Castro-Garcia approaches are dependent on crisis developments. Advocates or predictors of massive debt write-offs and swaps, whether they view the process as being initiated by forces within creditor or debtor countries, see a fundamental crisis about to emerge within LDCs. This crisis of political economy will either result in the repudiation of the debt by debtor countries, usually after the overthrow of democratic governments by radical political forces, or in the preemption of such repudiation and instability when creditor countries take the initiative to write down and forgive the debt. As Benjamin Weiner recently observed,

> Fidel Castro is right. The third world debt should be renounced. However, it is the United States that should take the initiative and unilaterally forgive the debt. By realistically acknowledging what is by now inevitable, we could preclude or limit the financial chaos and political grudges that would follow abrupt defaults by one or several of the major debtor nations.[61]

Fortune magazine echoes this observation.

> The main question for the banks is not whether their loans will be written down, but how that will be accomplished. The banks seem to have a choice: keeping up the pressure on the debtors or becoming more conciliatory. If the banks keep bearing down, repudiations seem sure to cripple the loan—Peru-style repudiations, if no other. Alternatively, if the bankers were willing to drop the round-tripping charade, they could cap their losses and also begin to bargain with debtors, ratcheting down the debt to levels the countries can more likely handle.[62]

A number of arguments can be made to demonstrate why these two scenarios are less likely to occur than the one depicting a successful case-by-case approach. First, the most likely scenario for OECD growth, oil prices, interest rates, and trade protectionism creates an external environment for debtor countries that is more conducive to giving something like the Baker plan a fair chance to work than it is for fostering political instability and debt repudiations within LDCs. Alternatively, a worst-case scenario of stagnant OECD growth, a new oil shock, rising interest rates, and massive trade barriers is quite unlikely.

Second, according to our analysis of political risk within BAM, not one of these major debtors has a high potential for political instability. The two with moderate instability ratings, Brazil and Argentina, have strengthened their systems by becoming more politically developed through higher levels of participation. Mexico, on the other hand, continues to practice statist politics under a liberal democratic facade. In an economic climate of austerity and massive debt, outbursts of participatory frustration have occurred in Mexico, particularly in provinces and towns bordering the United States. Nevertheless, Mexico's basic sociopolitical structures exhibit an overall low potential for instability. Political violence in Mexico, therefore, should be easily contained and only sporadic.

A third point that reduces the probability of these crisis-dependent scenarios from occurring concerns the political difficulty that governments would face in implementing these scenarios. In this sense the Bradley plan is flawed in a number of respects. For the Bradley plan to work far more questionable developments than those of the Baker plan would need to occur. First, banks would either have to accept or incur huge losses out of enlightened self-interest, or their governments would have to force them to do so. Second, debtor countries, once given massive debt relief, would still have to implement painful adjustment programs. This last point is key because without such an implementation, debtor countries' ability even to live up to the new and generous debt packages would be doubtful. Other debt write-off schemes, such as Felix Rohatyn's proposal to have the World Bank or another international agency buy LDC debt from commercial banks at a discount, suffer less from the uncertainty of true adjustment programs being implemented within LDCs than they do from the fact that the political support within OECD countries for such an indirect bailout of the banks does not exist.

Debt repudiation, moreover, for most countries, or for most political elites, is not a feasible and sustainable solution to their economic problems. This is particularly true for the democratic or quasi-democratic governments of BAM. Debt repudiation would run a high risk of severe, short-term economic problems. Such a development would naturally exacerbate the instability potential of these countries, especially given their large debts and democratic-like governments. Unlike Peru, the amount of debt that would be repudiated by any one of the BAM countries is too massive for commercial bankers to ignore. Declarations of default by banks, and the subsequent drying up of all trade credits and the seizing of the country's foreign assets, would probably result. An international economic crisis would follow. Very few political leaders would be willing to jump into such an abyss. As a result, major debt problems in the past have been negotiated and not generally subject to confrontational politics, and this pattern is likely to continue in the future. Thus, of the two crisis-dependent scenarios, a Bradley-like plan receives a higher probability of occurring, about 30 percent, versus a Castro-Garcia type of repudiation, the least likely of all three scenarios.

The strategic impact of these scenario projections on banks is fairly clear. For money-center banks and large regional banks with high LDC exposure, strong support for the Baker plan is necessary to further lower the chances of the other two scenarios occurring. For these major international banks, the formula still holds that the benefits of new loans plus the outstanding principal on old loans to the same borrower multiplied by the reduction in the probability of default brought about by the new commitment exceeds the costs of new loans plus the amount of new money loaned multiplied by the probability that a default will occur anyway after new lending.[63] For small regionals, on the other hand, with far less LDC exposure, the Baker plan may provide them the opportunity to get out of new loan packages, enabling a faster reduction in their overall risk position. Of course, big international banks that would contribute to Baker plan packages need to redouble efforts to reduce their increased exposure in debtor countries relative to their capital or asset base. No matter which of the three scenarios develop, international banks may be destined to take major hits on their profit-and-loss statements. Interest payments and their contribution to annual earnings will probably decrease one way or the other. Reduced earnings from LDC interest payments are likely results, whether from Baker-plan deals, Bradley-type write downs, or Peru-style repudiations.

SCENARIOS FOR MULTINATIONAL CORPORATIONS

The future role of multinational corporations in the world political economy has been a highly controversial subject for many years. Disagreements on this issue are very often ideological.[64] Extreme positions range from those who see multinationals as inevitable, irreversible, and steadily growing entities[65] to those who predict their ultimate decline or destruction through either government intervention and controls[66] or class-based revolution.[67] Others have a more problematic viewpoint, symbolized by the last passage in Raymond Vernon's classic work, *Sovereignty at Bay*.

> The basic asymmetry between multinational enterprises and national governments may be tolerable up to a point, but beyond that point there is need to re-establish balance. When this occurs, the response is bound to have some of the elements of the world corporation concept: accountability to some body, charged with weighing the activities of the multinational enterprise against a set of social yardsticks that are multinational in scope. If this does not happen, some of the apocalyptic projections of the future of multinational enterprise will grow more plausible.[68]

Vernon thus views the future of multinationals on the basis of probabilities. Either an international organization to regulate government-business conflicts and relations is created or the probability of an apocalyptic demise or decline of multinationals increases. It should be stressed, however, that the issue of so regulating multinationals is inextricably linked to the issue of a New International Economic Order (NIEO), both historically and in a more abstract, theoretical sense.

Historically, the control of multinationals by host governments and certain international agencies was a major part of the NIEO declaration passed by the U.N. General Assembly in 1974. This point of view, of course, primarily reflected the wishes of LDCs within the Group of 77. Although the power of this group has waned, it is still a powerful force in the debate.

Theoretically, it can be argued that the achievement of a viable international system of regulation is impossible without near-simultaneous agreements in other vitally important areas, such as trade and monetary reform, which are closely linked to the issue of a multinational regulatory system. Different interests, viewpoints, and issue linkages make consensus on regulations dependent on the resolution of the entire range of major international economic disputes, perhaps including the international debt crisis. The primary reasons for such linkages are twofold: all parties must be aware of the full package in order to assess and accept its effects, and a comprehensive settlement allows substantially more room for compromise and flexibility in negotiations. By the same token, the regulatory system must also be comprehensive (applied to all relevant aspects of multinational corporation and government behavior), have arbitration power, and be generally satisfactory to all affected parties, including most multinationals.[69] It seems that a multinational regulatory system and a concomitant NIEO will be possible only if multinationals take the initiative (and sacrifices) for its creation.[70]

The following discussion will explore the differing ideological perspectives on the future of multinationals in more detail. After describing each viewpoint, those whose projections are judged to have the highest probability of occurring will be analyzed, although no exact probabilities will be given. Such is the purest form of scenario development.

The first step in such an exercise is an analysis of different ideological beliefs along fundamental issues of political economy. This ideological examination of international relations can be seen in two major works, Robert Gilpin's *U.S. Power and the Multinational Corporation* and David Blake's and Robert Walter's *The Politics of Global Economic Relations*.[71] Most fundamentally, as seen in these works, each ideology has a particular viewpoint concerning the interrelationship of politics and economics, both normative and empirical. In large part the way an ideology frames this interrelationship shapes or predetermines perspectives on issues related to international trade and investment. In assessing the works and ideas of different theorists concerning international political economy, five separate ideologies emerge, as shown in Table 37.

Robert Cox analyzed five ideologies as they related to the NIEO and multinational corporations.[72] Our discussion, however, adopts only four of Cox's categories: the modern-monopolistic liberals; neomercantilists; social democrats; and Marxists, whom he termed "historical materialists." His fifth ideology, the "Third World Viewpoint," is really an extension of any of three ideologies cited above, the leftist neomercantilist; Marxist with a Maoist interpretation; or social democratic, like Mahbub ul Haq. Our discussion's fifth ideology is neoclassical liberalism, conspicuously absent from Cox's article. (In fact Cox made a major error by associating Harry Johnson with the modern-monopolistic perspective.) Johnson more aptly fits the neoclassical liberal ideology, which corresponds to Blake's and Walter's "classical economic liberal" and Gilpin's "sovereignty-at-bay" model.[73]

The best modern representative of neo-classical liberalism is Harry Johnson. His basic political-economic viewpoint concerns the predominance of economics over politics, that is, that economics should dominate or shape politics decisions. Neo-classical liberals see economic supremacy in both normative and empirical terms; they agree that fundamental market principles will, in the long run, maximize global wealth and prosperity. Policies and actions that seem to contribute to the maximization of pure market forces are termed economically rational, whereas political intrusions that negate market trends are viewed as irrational.

Neoclassical liberals, therefore, argue that government or political institutions should only serve to support or encourage the operation of markets. This necessitates a degree of international organization and coercion like that seen in GATT and the IMF to achieve maximization of free trade through the operation of comparative advantage theory, as Johnson has argued. Unlike modern-monopolistic liberals and social democrats, however, who are favorably disposed toward market principles but who also tend to support non-market-oriented political decisions, such as integrated commodity agreements or a general system

Table 37
Ideologies and the NIEO

Ideology	Political Economy		Economics	Politics	Value Goal/NIEO	Selected Representatives
Neo-classical liberals	economics	politics	maximize free markets	minimize and decentralize government	maximize global wealth/world corporatism	Harry Johnson John Diebold
Marxists	economics	politics	historical materialism and the class struggle	political-legal superstructure	maximize proletarian interests via revolution/global communism	Arghiri Emmanuel V. I. Lenin
Neo-mercantilists	economics	politics	wealth conflicts between nation-states	competition for power and nation-state survival	maximize national interests/power politics	Robert Gilpin Michael Hudson
Modern-monopolistic liberals	economics	politics	Keynesian economics	welfare-state politics	modest NIEO/ "management of interdependence"	Zbigniew Brzezinski G. Fred Bingsten
Social democrats	economics	politics	market socialism	government centralization and public ownership of monopolies	transformational NIEO/world government	Willy Brandt Jan Tinbergen

of tariff preferences (GSP), neoclassical liberals are rigidly opposed to any deviation from their conception of economic rationality. To them, the NIEO should be one of world corporatism supported by international organizations committed to free-trade-capital movements within an environment of stable, predictable, and relatively fixed exchange rates.[74]

Like neoclassical liberals, Marxists view economic forces as predominant over politics. But neoclassical liberals see economic forces leading society to progressively higher levels of wealth in a dynamic equilibrium, whereas Marxists view history as materialistically predetermined and propelled through inevitable stages by dialectics of class struggle, causing dynamic disequilibrium. The two ideologies' utopian visions or goals differ dramatically, even though economics is the primary driving force in their respective economically deterministic theories.

For Marxists the global political economy will inevitably evolve into worldwide communism. Indeed, recent events in the western political economy could be seen as confirming Marxist ideology. Growing strains within the western alliance are most serious in the economic area and concern a variety of issues, such as trade protectionism, monetary reform, raw material access, and increasingly competitive multinational corporations based in different countries. Lenin roughly outlined this scenario in his famous work, *Imperialism: The Final Stage of Capitalism*.[75] In terms of North-South relations and developments within the Third World, the notion that rapid capitalistic penetration of underdeveloped countries quickens the revolutionary process (as Marx argued about the British impact on India, in particular, or as Arghiri Emmanuel pointed out recently in more general, theoretical terms)[76] could be supported by recent events, given rising radical revolutions throughout the developing world, represented most dramatically by the Iranian and Nicaraguan revolutions. The almost total shift in the direction and value goals of the Non-Alignment Movement in Havana in 1979 concretely demonstrates this radicalization process. The international debt crisis, moreover, could prove fertile ground for an upsurge in such radical political movement, as Castro hopes.

Some neomercantilists share many of the Marxists' conclusions about the short-term probabilities or prospects for the international political economy. For example, Robert Gilpin, Michael Hudson, David Calleo, and Benjamin Rowland agree that the decline of U.S. military, political, and economic hegemony in the 1970s has caused growing competitive economic nationalism among the United States, Western Europe, and Japan. They also see the future decline of the multinational corporation in such a competitive nation-state environment as inevitable.[77] This analysis is based primarily on the assumption that past historical patterns will hold in the future, that is, that high levels of free trade and capital movements by international businesses require the political-military dominance of one nation-state (e.g., Great Britain in the nineteenth century and the United States in the immediate post–World War II period). In basic terms, neomercantilists have a viewpoint of the relationship between economics and politics directly opposite that of the neoclassical liberals and Marxists, namely that nation-states striving for power and survival ultimately determine the structure of economic relationships.

Such a perspective on political economy results in the neomercantilists having a different viewpoint from Marxists on the consequences of growing economic nationalism between developed countries. Instead of global proletarian revolution, neomercantilists see growing regionalism resulting in greater development and prosperity for nearly all concerned developed and Third World countries. This, however, requires U.S. leadership and recognition of the realities of world power patterns leading to the inevitability of regionalism. In essence what Gilpin, Hudson, Calleo, and Rowland advocate is the creation of cooperative regional blocs, an international system Gilpin called "benign mercantilism." The only other prospect was "malevolent mercantilism"—highly competitive, uncooperative relations between all nation-states leading to economic chaos and possibly war.[78]

An international organization was formed largely in response to growing neomercantilist trends in the late 1960s and early 1970s. This organization, known as the Trilateral Commission, symbolized the character of the fourth ideology's position toward the NIEO. It was formed in late 1971 on the initiative of David Rockefeller and other associates within Bildenberger circles in response to the "Nixon shocks" of August 1971 and the introduction of the protectionistic Burke-Hartke Trade Bill within the U.S. Congress in September of that year. Rockefeller is reputed to have been inspired by Zbigniew Brzezinski's 1970 publication, *Between Two Ages* and appointed Brzezinski the Trilateral Commission's chairman.[79]

The major works of the Trilateral Commission and related Council on Foreign Relations on North-South issues were written by Richard Gardner, et al., Richard Cooper, et al., Roger Hansen, Albert Fishlow, G. Fred Bergsten, and Jagdish Bhagwati.[80] All share the same basic "modern-monopolistic liberal" perspective on North-South relations and the NIEO: growing pressures for protectionism and regionalism are the chief threats to a critically needed NIEO incorporating all major North-South nation-states into structurally reformed and more powerful international organizations. Such organizations would be dedicated to fostering trade liberalization within integrated commodity-GSP agreements and to eliminating absolute poverty in the developing world over time. Encouraging a proper investment climate for multinational corporations in developing countries, moreover, is coupled with the goal to create broader, more effective international regulations over their behavior. By coordinating the policies of developed countries and co-opting major Southern states into genuine positions of power in reformed international organizations, the "management of interdependence" is possible and is in the best interests of all concerned parties.

The key concept of the modern-monopolistic position is interdependence and its perceived consequences. Mutual dependencies, the essence of the interdependence concept, create mutual vulnerabilities and potential nation-state tensions that generate domestic protectionistic pressures. If neomercantilism becomes politically dominant, all parties concerned will suffer the economic consequences of stagflation. Thus interdependence must be maintained and managed in a way that reaches a compromise between the political forces of nationalism and the economic rationality of basic free trade and capital movements internationally, epitomized by the activities of multinational corporations. Such a compromise requires an integrated approach including structural reform of international organizations, new rules governing trade, monetary, and investment issues, coordination of OECD policies in these matters, cooperation of major LDC states in the NIEO, and a strong commitment to the "basic needs approach."[81]

Modern-monopolistic liberals, therefore, have a highly interactive view of political economy, seeing both political and economic forces as basically equivalent in importance and needing to be dealt with simultaneously. That is, the chief goal of the NIEO is to find "a range of livable compromises between the legitimate claims of national sovereignty and the imperatives of international [economic] order."[82]

A final ideological perspective on the NIEO, the social democratic viewpoint, also promotes a highly integrated view of politics and economics. Social democrats and modern-monopolistic liberals essentially differ regarding the normative political and economic consequences of this observed interaction. Politically, social democrats have much greater commitment to "participatory democracy," whereas modern-monopolistic liberals tend to be "pluralist democrats." Accordingly, social democrats are less concerned with adverse domestic political reactions in OECD countries as a major potential obstacle to the NIEO than are modern-monopolistic liberals.[83]

This perspective, with its faith in broad-based democratic participation, results in a more flexible, less constrained position on the exact nature and transformational character of the NIEO. Economic and political proposals of social democrats for the NIEO are much more transformational than modern-monopolistic liberals in several respects: political reforms are proposed to propel the global system toward world government; the relative power of LDCs in these world-governmentlike institutions is viewed to be much greater than the more modest NIEO envisioned by Trilateralites; a much stronger financial commitment to the basic-needs approach is evident; and the monopoly/oligopoly character of multinational corporations requires more public ownership and control.

Three major social democratic works are *Reshaping the International Order (RIO)*, by Jan Tinbergen, et al., *The Poverty Curtain*, by Majbub ul Haq, and *North-South: A Programme for Survival*, by Willy Brandt, et al.[84] The last two address many deficiencies found in Tinbergen, such as a lack of political sensitivity to domestic political restraints within OECD countries and a failure to present reasonable tactical approaches to transformational goals.

The Brandt report is especially good in dealing with this problem, but it has been widely criticized and rejected by most OECD elites.[85] Essentially, the Brandt report attempts to reach a basic compromise between the major demands of the South and the political constraints in the North within a social democratic perspective. In the process it opens itself to criticism from both sides, as the generally negative LDC reaction has matched the cold reception among OECD countries. Perhaps this reaction suggests that although the Brandt proposals may have some merit, serious consideration of them will not take place unless the world political economy enters into a period of systemic crisis and breakdown.

Thus ideological conceptions of the general nature of political economy shape views of the future of multinational corporations. In effect all ideologies see different kinds of NIEOs emerging in the evolving global political economy. These contending perspectives, moreover, can be analyzed in terms of scenarios.

One possible scenario concerns the creation of an NIEO along the lines of the modern-monopolistic liberal ideology. Although such an NIEO's impact on multinationals would vary with the type of firm (e.g., raw-material-based firms versus high-technology, consumer-oriented firms), an analysis in terms of general multinational interests is still valid. In fact certain NIEOs could further the growth and profits of most multinationals.[86] This in itself could be a strong incentive to initiate and support the creation of a NIEO to improve and stabilize the global business climate. Indeed, nearly all international agreements reached thus far regarding multinational-related regulations have been supported, if not initiated, by business. This includes international tax treaties and guidelines and the 1976 OECD code related to multinational and government behavior.[87] Effective and productive agreements in this area in the future will require multinational support, if not initiation.

Other motivations exist as well for multinational action toward the NIEO. According to Vernon, ending jurisdictional conflicts, which Vernon sees as a serious problem escalating in intensity, could only be accomplished if an "international regime" adjudicating such conflicts was created.[88] Most, if not all, multinational corporations fear the situation Dresser Industries faced in the Soviet-pipeline controversy.

Another motivation concerns the monetary reform that could be expected in an NIEO. A return to a fixed exchange rate system (not based on gold) would probably accompany the attainment of comprehensive international economic agreements in trade and on multinationals. A return to a fixed system is strongly advocated by nearly all NIEO proponents.[89] International monetary developments over the past few years have been too volatile and have exacerbated international tensions. Trade and investment flows have been affected as a result. In particular multinational corporations have been adversely affected by the large, volatile, and unpredictable fluctuations in foreign-exchange markets. Certainly, in the view of modern-monopolistic liberals, governments and the international business community have a mutual incentive to substantially reform the present exchange rate system or, at the very least, control its operation.

An NIEO would also include comprehensive trade reforms. The intensifying trade tensions within the OECD community and between OECDs and LDCs are perhaps the most dangerous threat to multinational operations. An NIEO would most likely eliminate this threat, and such a process could be linked to the resolution of the international debt crisis, as proposed by the Bradley plan.

Regardless of any logic or reason, sufficient support for an NIEO and a deep commitment to endure sacrifices based on the necessity of compromise by all major parties (OECD countries, LDCs, and multinationals) is unlikely to emerge in the foreseeable future. Thus in the medium term, 1986–91, the rising threat of a more dangerous neomercantilist world could be anticipated. If so, multinational corporations should plan accordingly by divestment or retrenchment of many marginal FDIs, by emphasizing liquidity in financial decisions and goals, and by integrating environmental scanning into a systematic strategic planning process.[90] U.S.-based multinationals, moreover, should probably focus FDI expansion, if any, in certain North and Latin American countries, which constitute part of the U.S.-dominated subsystem outlined in Gilpin's benign mercantilist model.

In the longer term (ten to twenty years), achievement of an NIEO along the lines of modern-monopolistic liberalism is more likely. Nevertheless it could only be achieved if the international debt crisis is successfully resolved and if multinationals give strong support to the effort. Jack Behrman, in fact, argued that the consequence of not taking such an initiative (which he predicted due to an unwillingness among multinationals to voluntarily disclose a sufficient amount of corporate data to government bodies)[91] "is likely to be an increase in disintegration of the world economy through national governments turning inward or forming tight regional associations, excluding the efficiency seeker type of company in favor of the market seeker."[92]

Efficiency seekers ideally attempt to make and maintain FDIs that are rational and efficient in terms of comparative-advantage theory. Multiple markets are then served through inter- and intra-firm trade. Market seekers, however, tend to serve only separate national markets and thus reduce specialization in trade and production. Thus the suboptimal transformation of many multinationals into separate, uncoordinated national or state-controlled firms would take place. Centralized activities would then tend to be dominated by pure marketing and service organizations. This would be the direct consequence of a more uncertain and hostile international business environment, as Richard Robinson recently predicted.[93]

Admittedly, other scholars sympathetic to multinational-initiated regulations because of the neomercantilist threat do not see the future in terms of the Behrman scenario. Vernon, for example, seems to think that host and home governments will realize over time that accommodation is preferable to the economic consequences of protectionism.[94] Thus Vernon, at least by implication, thinks the creation of an international business regulation system will take place only after governments, especially LDCs, take the initiative to settle their disputes with multinationals. Of course, efforts to resolve the debt crisis might be the catalyst to change LDC policies and attitudes toward multinationals. Howard Perlmutter,

Herman Kahn, and Charles Kindleberger seem to share this general viewpoint.[95] Vernon, however, does not dismiss the possibility of events that would be "apocalyptic" for multinationals. He simply dismisses the probability of this happening as being significantly lower than his favored scenario. Behrman, Gilpin, Joan Spero, and Warren Keegan, on the other hand, tend to charge that this view vastly underestimates several factors: the power of nationalism, especially during times of nation-state crisis; the potential capacity of governments to control business in very stifling ways; and the often economic irrationality associated with purely political decisions, which seem to dominate much government activity.

A middle scenario between the Vernon and Behrman groups seems equally, if not more, plausible. One could argue that capitulation by either government or business, in which one must essentially surrender their best interests to the other, is unlikely. Both have sufficient power resources to survive attacks from the other. Nation-states will continue to control the terms of access to their territories, and today's MNCs are qualitatively and quantitatively different from those business organizations that declined dramatically in the late nineteenth and early twentieth centuries. Besides greater multinational financial resources and centralized control based on modern transportation and communication systems, nation-states face additional constraints in formulating mercantilist-like international economic and business policies. For LDCs successfully resolving the debt crisis will most likely require a more open foreign investment climate. For OECD countries the historical experience of the 1930s plus the common Soviet threat mitigate the kinds of "beggar-thy-neighbor" policies that precipitously reduced multinational activity after the decline of British dominance. The end of U.S. hegemony in the post–World War II era, thus, will not have the same impact on international business that the previous British decline had. Most dire neomercantilist predictions are based on the assumption that this historical pattern will be duplicated.

In this sense government and international business should be viewed as rather permanent organizations having interests in "complementary competition."[96] Their interests are neither totally compatible nor antagonistic. Labor-management relations offer a good analogy, for each party needs the other, and failure to negotiate a mutually satisfactory arrangement is detrimental to both. A substantial middle ground thus exists between reaching an agreement that means government policy is virtually dictated by business or one that requires business to fully open financial-technical information for public-government scrutiny. Either kind of capitulation is highly improbable.

There is a strong likelihood, therefore, that in the next two decades international business–government relations will continue to be one of complimentary competition between two fairly autonomous entities. The exact quality and nature of these relations will depend largely on the success or failure of negotiations and political risk management. For international banks, the primary issue is the successful resolution of the debt crisis, which will continue to require astute, far-reaching negotiations. For nonfinancial multinationals, competitive survival will require an increase in their international operations and a perspective based on the globalization of markets.[97]

Many industries (automobiles, tires, computers, plastics-resins, soft drinks, aerospace, construction machinery, and televisions) are already global in nature; firms with one-third or more of total sales outside their home country have at least one-third of the world market share.[98] Most other industries are rapidly becoming global. Perhaps even more importantly, industries that OECD countries dominate and increasingly emphasize, based on the "electronics complex," are already global in nature because their high unit-value-to-weight ratios encourage international trade, their knowledge-service intensity allows more flexibility in investment-location decisions, and their high technological innovation and spread requires firms to chase the international product life cycle more rapidly.[99] Thus the migration of multinational corporations from OECDs to LDCs should accelerate in the foreseeable future. One study estimates that LDCs will produce 25 percent of world industrial value-added products at the turn of the century, as compared with only 12 percent in 1970.[100] Entrance into these countries, however, will not be automatic, whether corporations, host governments, or an international body dictate the rules of entry and operation. It is more likely that entry decisions and multinational operations will be judged on a case-by-case basis and will, therefore, be subject to negotiation. Of course, successful entries and operations are usually mutually beneficial to both the corporation and the host government.

Initiatives for reaching government-business accommodations are not the primary responsibility of either party over the other but of both. On the part of business—both banking and industrial—several actions can be recommended. Most basic is a needed redirection of business school and corporate training programs toward a greater awareness of public policy concerns and issues. Only through such awareness can business leaders be effective negotiators with and participants in the political process. Corporate lobbying activity should be intensified and geared more explicitly toward general and collective interests that go beyond individual firm needs. The Trilateral Commission is a contemporary example of a banking-industrial-government combine that should be extended, broadened, and duplicated by others. More political action committee funds and efforts should be directed toward the achievement of collective business-government goals as opposed to traditionally pursued objectives that are firm- or industry-specific. Without such corporate/business school efforts to find mutually acceptable public policies, the general economic climate for business may suffer and deteriorate. In this sense a paradox exists. Government-business relations are both the problem and the solution to the systemic crisis that the international political economy now faces.

NOTES

1. Herman Kahn and A. J. Wiener, *The Year 2000* (New York: Macmillan, 1967), pp. 262–64.

2. P. W. Beck, ''Corporate Planning for an Uncertain Future,'' *Long Range Planning* 15, no. 4, 1982, p. 13.

3. See Leslie E. Grayson, *How and Who in Planning for Large Companies* (London: Macmillan, 1986) and The Colgate Darden Graduate School of Business case, *Scenario Planning*, Leslie E. Grayson, UVA-G-260, 1985, p. 5.

4. Stephen J. Kobrin, John Basek, Stephen Blank, and Joseph La Palombara, ''The Assessment and Evaluation of Noneconomic Environments by American Firms: A Preliminary Report,'' *Journal of International Business Studies*, Spring-Summer 1980, p. 40.

5. Robert Grosse and John Stock, ''Noneconomic Risk Evaluation in Multinational Banks,'' *Management International Review* 24, no. 1, 1984, p. 46.

6. The following recommended approach is largely based on the system used and developed by one multinational oil company; see W. P. Rossiter, R. S. Karplus and N. Jones, ''Managing for the Future: The Scenario Technique,'' Conoco internal memorandum, Wilmington, Del., 1984, discussed in Grayson, *Scenario Planning*, pp. 7, 27–28.

7. William H. Overholt, ''The Scenario Technique,'' *Political Risks in International Business: New Directions for Research, Management, and Public Policy*, Thomas L. Brewer, ed. (New York: Praeger Publishers, 1985), p. 153.

8. Grayson, *Scenario Planning*, p. 28.

9. Overholt, ''The Scenario Technique,'' p. 160.

10. Ibid., p. 161, and Grayson, *Scenario Planning*, p. 9.

11. Leopoldo Solis, ''Some Thoughts on Mexico's Foreign Indebtedness,'' *The World Economy*, March 1986, p. 72.

12. Morgan Guaranty Trust Company of New York, ''The Baker Initiative: The Perspective of the Banks,'' *World Financial Markets*, February 1986, p. 7.

13. Morgan Guaranty Trust Company of New York, ''Strengthening the LDC Debt Strategy,'' *World Financial Markets*, September/October 1985, p. 11.

14. William R. Cline, ''International Debt and the Stability of the World Economy,'' *Policy Analysis in International Economics*, no. 4, September 1983.

15. William R. Cline, ''International Debt: From Crisis to Recovery?'' *The American Economic Review*, May 1985, p. 186.

16. Ibid., p. 188.

17. Ibid., p. 187.

18. Ibid., pp. 187–88.

19. Morgan Guaranty Trust Company of New York, ''The Baker Initiative: The Perspective of the Banks,'' *World Financial Markets*, February 1986, p. 3.

20. The International Monetary Fund, *World Economic Outlook*, April 1986, p. 99.

21. Ibid., pp. 94–101.

22. Ibid., pp. 96–97.

23. Cline, ''From Crisis to Recovery,'' p. 185.

24. *World Economic Outlook*, April 1986, p. 89.

25. Eduardo Wiesner, ''Latin American Debt: Lessons and Pending Issues,'' *The American Economic Review*, May 1985, p. 191.

26. *World Economic Outlook*, April 1986, p. 101.

27. James Baker, quoted by Raoul D. Edwards, ''The World Debt Crisis and the Baker Plan,'' *United States Banker*, April 1986, p. 54.

28. *World Financial Markets*, February 1986, p. 6.

29. Baker, *United States Banker*, pp. 54, 90.

30. Ibid., p. 54.

31. Christopher Johnson, "Fleshing Out the Baker Plan for Third World Debt," *The Banker*, December 1985, p. 16.

32. Baker, *United States Banker*, p. 54.

33. *The Wall Street Journal*, September 10, 1985, p. 30; and *The Wall Street Journal*, September 16, 1985, p. 46.

34. Martin Feldstein, "From Crisis to Renewed Growth," *Challenge*, July-August 1984, p. 27.

35. *World Economic Outlook*, April 1986, pp. 100–101.

36. Bill Bradley, quoted in *The Washington Post*, July 6, 1986, p. K5.

37. Ibid.

38. Ibid., p. K1.

39. Ibid.

40. Ibid., p. K5; *The Washington Post*, April 10, 1986, p. A14; *Fortune*, December 23, 1985, pp. 98–102; and Rudiger Dornbusch, "Policy and Performance Links between LDC Debtors and Industrial Nations," *Brookings Papers on Economic Activity*, no. 2, 1985, pp. 303–56.

41. Dornbusch, "Policy and Performance Links," pp. 337–38.

42. Ibid., p. 336.

43. Ibid., p. 338.

44. Ibid., p. 346.

45. Ibid., p. 348.

46. Rudiger Dornbusch, "The Latin American Dimension," *Challenge*, July-August 1984, p. 11.

47. Dornbusch, "Policy and Performance Links," pp. 352–53.

48. Bradley, *The Washington Post*, p. K5.

49. Fidel Castro, quoted in *The Wall Street Journal*, June 12, 1985, p. 30.

50. Fidel Castro, quoted in *The Economist*, August 17, 1985, p. 13.

51. For one specific recommendation of how debtor countries should jointly and unilaterally change the approach to the debt crisis, see David Felix, "How to Resolve Latin American's Debt Crisis," *Challenge*, November-December 1985, pp. 44–51.

52. *Fortune*, December 23, 1985, pp. 100–102.

53. Cline, "From Crisis to Recovery," p. 185; and Dornbusch, "Policy and Performance Links," pp. 337–38.

54. *Economic Report of the President*, February 1985, p. 356; and *Economic Report of the President*, February 1986, p. 378.

55. Anthony M. Soloman, "LDC Debt: Where Do We Go from Here?" *The Banker*, August 1985, pp. 16–17.

56. William Cline, quoted in *The Wall Street Journal*, May 26, 1983, p. 34; and IMF, *World Economic Outlook*, April 1986, p. 98.

57. *The Wall Street Journal*, September 10, 1985, p. 30.

58. *World Economic Outlook*, April 1986, p. 94.

59. *World Financial Markets*, February 1986, p. 6.

60. Bill Bradley, quoted in *The Washington Post*, July 23, 1986, p. G1.

61. Benjamin Weiner, "End the Charade on Third World Debt," *The New York Times*, May 18, 1986, p. F3.

62. *Fortune*, December 23, 1986, p. 102.

63. William R. Cline, "Changing Stresses on the World Economy," *The World Economy*, June 1985, p. 140.

64. For examples, see Robert W. Cox, "Ideologies and the New International Economic Order: Reflections on Some Recent Literature," *International Organization* 33, no. 2, Spring 1979, pp. 257–99; and Robert Gilpin, *U.S. Power and the Multinational Corporation: The Political Economy of Foreign Direct Investment* (New York: Basic Books, 1975), pp. 213–62.

65. Harry Johnson, *International Economic Questions Facing Britain, the United States, and Canada in the Seventies*, British-North American Research Association, London, June 1970, p. 24; and John Diebold, "Multinational Corporations—Why Be Scared of Them?" *Foreign Policy*, no. 12, Fall 1973, pp. 79–95.

66. Gilpin, *U.S. Power*, pp. 253–62; and Michael Hudson, *Global Fracture: The New International Economic Order* (New York: Harper and Row, 1977), pp. 1–16; David Calleo and Benjamin Rowland, *America and the World Political Economy* (Bloomington: Indiana University Press, 1973), pp. 1–6, 251–59.

67. Paul A. Baran and Paul M. Sweezey, *Monopoly Capital* (Harmondsworth, Middlesex: Penguin, 1968), pp. 178–214; Samir Amin, "The World Crisis of the 1980s," *Monthly Review* 33, no. 2, June 1981, pp. 33–43; Harry Magdoff, *The Age of Imperialism* (New York: Monthly Review Press, 1969).

68. Raymond Vernon, *Sovereignty at Bay: The Multinational Spread of U.S. Enterprises* (New York: Basic Books, 1971), p. 284.

69. Miriam Camps, *Collective Management: The Reform of Global Economic Organizations*, 1980s Project/Council on Foreign Relations (New York: McGraw-Hill, 1981), pp. 134–52; Rainer Hellman, *Transitional Control of Multinational Corporations* (New York: Praeger Publishers, 1977), pp. 1–23; C. Fred Bergsten, Thomas Horst, and Theodore Moran, *American Multinationals and American Interests* (Washington, D.C.: The Brookings Institute, 1978), pp. 488–90.

70. Jack Behrman, "Transnational Corporations in the New International Economic Order," *Journal of International Business Studies*, Tenth Anniversary Special Issue, Spring-Summer 1981, pp. 39–42; Andre van Dam, "The Corporate Role in a North-South Dialogue," *Long Range Planning* 12, no. 6, December 1979, p. 25; Endel-Jakob Kolde, *Environment of International Business* (Boston: Kent Publishing Co., 1982), pp. 294–95; Warren Keegan, "The Future of the Multinational Manufacturing Corporation: Five Scenarios," *Journal of International Business Studies* 10, no. 1, Spring-Summer 1979, p. 104.

71. Gilpin, *U.S. Power*, pp. 20–43; and David H. Blake and Robert S. Walters, *The Politics of Global Economic Relations* (Englewood Cliffs, NJ: Prentice-Hall, 1976), pp. 1–10.

72. Cox, "Ideologies," pp. 261, 280–82.

73. Gilpin, *U.S. Power*, pp. 220–28; and Blake and Walters, *Politics*, pp. 5–6.

74. Harry Johnson, *International Trade and Economic Growth* (Cambridge, MA: Harvard University Press, 1958), pp. 31–55.

75. V. I. Lenin, *Imperialism: The Highest Stage of Capitalism* (New York: International Publishers, 1939), pp. 68–108.

76. Karl Marx, "The Future Results of British Rule in India," in *Karl Marx on Colonialism and Modernization*, Shlomo Avineri, ed. (New York: Doubleday, 1969), pp. 136–37; and Arghiri Emmanuel, "The Multinational Corporation and Inequality of Development," *International Social Science Journal* 28, no. 4, 1976, pp. 754–72.

77. Gilpin, *U.S. Power*, pp. 253–62; Hudson, *Global Fracture*, pp. 236–68; Calleo and Rowland, *America*, pp. 1–6, 251–59.

78. Calleo and Rowland, *America*, pp. 251–59; and Gilpin, *U.S. Power*, pp. 253–62.

79. Zbigniew Brzezinski, *Between Two Ages* (New York: Viking Press, 1970).

80. Richard N. Gardiner, Saburo Okita, and B. J. Udink, "A Turning Point in North-South Economic Relations," *The Triangle Papers: 3* (New York: The Trilateral Commission, 1974), pp. 57–74; Richard N. Cooper, Karl Kaiser, and Mastaka Kosaka, "Towards a Renovated International System," *The Triangle Papers: 14* (New York: The Trilateral Commission, 1977), pp. 34–42; Roger D. Hansen and Albert Fislow, *Rich and Poor Nations in the World Economy*, 1980s Project, Council on Foreign Relations (New York: McGraw-Hill, 1978), pp. 11–83, 217–54; G. Fred Bergsten, et al., *The Reform of International Institutions* (New York: The Trilateral Commission, 1976); and Jagdish N. Bhagwati, ed., *The New International Economic Order: The North-South Debate* (Cambridge, MA: MIT Press, 1977), pp. 2–24, 347–53.

81. Gardner, et al., "North-South," pp. 67–71; and Roger D. Hansen, "North-South Policy—What's the Problem?" *Foreign Affairs*, Summer 1980, pp. 1121–28.

82. Gaido Colonna di Paliano, Phillip Trexise, and Nobuhiko Ushiba, "Directions for World Trade in the 1970s," *The Triangle Papers: 4* (New York: The Trilateral Commission, 1974), pp. 77–98.

83. For the major Trilateral Commission report on political democracy, see Michael Crozier, Samuel Huntington, and Joji Watanuki, *The Crisis of Democracy: Report on the Governability of Democracies to the Trilateral Commission* (New York: New York University Press, 1975).

84. Jan Tinbergen, *Reshaping the International Order: A Report to the Club of Rome* (New York: E. P. Dutton, 1976); Mahbub ul Haq, *The Poverty Curtain: Choices for the Third World* (New York: New York University Press, 1976); Willy Brandt, et al., *North-South: A Programme for Survival*, Report of the International Commission on International Development Issues (Cambridge, MA: MIT Press, 1980).

85. Miguel S. Wionczek, "The Brandt Report," *Third World Quarterly*, January 1981, p. 105; Graham Bird, "The Controversial Economics of the Brandt Report," *The World Today*, December 1980, pp. 463–68; Melvin B. Krauss, "Brandt Report Is Irrelevant to Third World," *The Wall Street Journal*, August 28, 1980.

86. Van Dam, "Corporate Role," p. 24.

87. Raymond Vernon, "Sovereignty at Bay Ten Years After," *International Organization* 35, no. 3, Summer 1981, p. 527; and John G. Crean, "Guidelines and Codes for Multinational Enterprises," *CA Magazine*, March 1980, pp. 61–62.

88. Vernon, "Ten Years After," p. 526.

89. For example, see Cooper, Kaiser, and Kosaka, "Towards a Renovated International System," pp. 34–42; and Brandt, *North-South: A Programme for Survival*, pp. 201–20.

90. Peter F. Drucker, *Managing in Turbulent Times* (New York: Harper and Row, 1980), pp. 1–71, 153–221.

91. Behrman, "Transnational Corporations," pp. 40–41.

92. Ibid., p. 40.

93. Richard Robinson, "Background Concepts and Philosophy of International Business from World War II to the Present," *Journal of International Business Studies*, Tenth Anniversary Special Issue, Spring-Summer 1981, pp. 16–21.

94. Vernon, "Ten Years After," pp. 527–29.

95. Herman Kahn, *World Economic Development: 1979 and Beyond* (New York:

Morrow Quill, 1979), pp. 248–52; Charles Kindleberger, *American Business Abroad* (New Haven: Yale University Press, 1969), pp. 201–07; and Howard Perlmatter, "A View of the Future," *The New Sovereigns*, Abdul A. Said and Luiz Simmons, eds. (Englewood Cliffs, NJ: Prentice-Hall, 1975), pp. 167–86.

96. Samuel P. Huntington, "Transnational Corporations in World Politics," *World Politics*, April 1973, pp. 333–67.

97. Michael E. Porter, "Changing Patterns of International Competition," *California Management Review*, Winter 1986, pp. 9–40; and Theodore Levitt, "The Globalization of Markets," *Harvard Business Review*, May-June 1983, pp. 92–102.

98. William H. Davidson, *Global Strategic Management* (New York: John Wiley and Sons, 1982), p. 7.

99. Franklin Root, "Some Trends in the World Economy and Their Implications for International Business Strategy," *Journal of International Business Studies*, Winter 1984, pp. 21–22.

100. OECD, *Facing the Future*, Paris, 1979, p. 88.

APPENDIX A

Glossary for Sociopolitical Variables

1. *Social diversity* is the number and size of distinct ethnic, tribal, religious, and regional groups in the society. The higher the diversity, the more unlikely the society can meet all the disparate needs and demands.
2. *Congruent cleavages* occur when distinct ethnic, tribal, religious, and regional groups overlap with the low or poor class. Such an overlap, particularly for a large group, is a strong cause of political instability.
3. *Income distribution* measures the degree of economic class inequities in society. The higher those inequities, the more potential for political instability.
4. The *political system* can be of four fundamental types: authoritarian-traditional (i.e., monarchy, or military warlord); authoritarian-mobilizational (i.e., totalitarianism); liberal-democratic (i.e., parliamentary or presidential) and newly independent (within a generation of being a colony). The most politically stable system is authoritarian-mobilizational, followed by liberal-democratic. Authoritarian-traditional systems are relatively unstable, but newly independent countries are the most unstable.
5. *Past internal war* is the occurrence of a major political upheaval within the last generation. Such upheaval could be civil war, revolution, or chronic military coups. The occurrence of past internal war sets the precedent or provides additional incentives for more instability.
6. *Elite repression* is the extent to which the government uses negative sanctions or physical force against the domestic population. Generally, a high level of state violence against its citizens increases the probability of political instability.
7. *Elite illegitimacy* develops when a significant or large number of the population no longer respects the authority of government rulers. The more people who have such feelings, the more likely the political system will be unstable.

8. *The role of the military* refers to the armed forces' present relationship to government rulers. If the military has the capability and will to change the government, then the political system is very unstable.
9. *The role of land reform* is related to economic sectoral transformations. In nearly all modernizing societies, an effective land reform program is essential for the stable transition from a predominantly agrarian to industrial society.

APPENDIX B

Political Risk Questionnaire: General Motors Corporation

____
COUNTRY

POLITICAL FACTORS

A. LEADERSHIP

1. Attitudes toward foreign investment and the automotive industry.

   NEGATIVE __ __ __ __ __ __ POSITIVE

2. The likelihood of leadership changes that will adversely affect auto investment.

   VERY LIKELY __ __ __ __ __ __ __ UNLIKELY

3. The predictability of government policy and behavior affecting the auto industry.

   UNPREDICTABLE __ __ __ __ __ __ __ PREDICTABLE

4. The reliability of the regime and the likelihood of sudden shifts in policy toward foreign automotive operations.

   UNRELIABLE __ __ __ __ __ __ __ RELIABLE

5. The degree of corruption among leadership groups.

   VERY CORRUPT __ __ __ __ __ __ __ LITTLE CORRUPTION

B. SOCIAL INTEGRATION

1. The degree of fragmentation in the society along ethnic, religious, class, regional, etc. lines.

   FRAGMENTED __ __ __ __ __ __ __ COHESIVE

2. The potential for social conflict among groups in the country.

   HIGH __ __ __ __ __ __ __ LOW

3. The degree of governmental repression and police state tactics.

HIGH __ __ __ __ __ __ __ LOW

4. The nature of income distribution.

UNEQUAL __ __ __ __ __ __ __ EQUAL

5. The attitude of the general populace toward foreigners.

HOSTILE__ __ __ __ __ __ __ FRIENDLY

C. <u>EXTERNAL INVOLVEMENT</u>

1. The likelihood of war with another country.

HIGH __ __ __ __ __ __ __ LOW

2. The likelihood of guerrilla/terrorist operations against the regime.

HIGH __ __ __ __ __ __ __ LOW

3. The degree of the country's involvement in international organizations.

HIGH __ __ __ __ __ __ __ LOW

4. The degree that the country participates in the world economy.

HIGH __ __ __ __ __ __ __ LOW

5. The likely effect of outside involvements on the auto industry (e.g. membership in economic associations).

NEGATIVE __ __ __ __ __ __ __ POSITIVE

____
COUNTRY

PART ONE: ASSESSMENT OF FACTORS

REGULATORY FACTORS

A. FINANCE

1. The likelihood of profit repatriation restrictions that will adversely affect the auto industry.

   HIGH __ __ __ __ __ __ __ LOW

2. The likelihood of adverse foreign exchange controls.

   HIGH __ __ __ __ __ __ __ LOW

3. The likelihood of adverse taxes on automotive investments.

   HIGH __ __ __ __ __ __ __ LOW

4. The likelihood of adverse controls on prices and/or credit affecting the auto industry.

   HIGH __ __ __ __ __ __ __ LOW

5. The likelihood of other adverse financial restrictions on foreign auto operations.

B. ENERGY

1. The likelihood that energy will be available.

   LOW __ __ __ __ __ __ __ HIGH

2. The likelihood that oil supplies will be secure.

   LOW __ __ __ __ __ __ __ HIGH

3. The likelihood that energy demand will be controlled by the government in a way that will adversely affect the auto industry.

   HIGH __ __ __ __ __ __ __ LOW

4. The likelihood of increased fuel efficiency requirements that will adversely effect the auto industry.

HIGH __ __ __ __ __ __ __ LOW

5. The likelihood that the country will experience other energy problems.

HIGH __ __ __ __ __ __ __ LOW

C. LABOR

1. The likelihood of adverse employment regulations.

HIGH __ __ __ __ __ __ __ LOW

2. The likelihood of adverse laws regarding unionization.

HIGH __ __ __ __ __ __ __ LOW

3. The likelihood of adverse bargaining restrictions.

HIGH __ __ __ __ __ __ __ LOW

4. The likelihood of adverse arbitration procedures.

HIGH __ __ __ __ __ __ __ LOW

5. The likelihood of other adverse labor conditions.

HIGH __ __ __ __ __ __ __ LOW

D. AUTOMOTIVE

1. The likelihood of local content laws.

HIGH __ __ __ __ __ __ __ LOW

2. The likelihood of adverse import controls.

HIGH __ __ __ __ __ __ __ LOW

3. The likelihood of adverse export controls.

HIGH __ __ __ __ __ __ __ LOW

4. The likelihood of undue indigenization requirements.

HIGH __ __ __ __ __ __ __ LOW

____
COUNTRY

PART ONE: ASSESSMENT OF FACTORS

POLICY FACTORS

A. DEVELOPMENT

1. The stage of development the country has reached.

   TRADITIONAL __ __ __ __ __ __ __ POSTINDUSTRIAL

2. The ability of the government to foster development.

   LOW __ __ __ __ __ __ __ HIGH

3. The success of the government at meeting development plans.

   LOW __ __ __ __ __ __ __ HIGH

4. The ability of the government to broaden political participation throughout the society

   LOW __ __ __ __ __ __ __ HIGH

5. The anticipated role of the auto industry in development.

   UNIMPORTANT __ __ __ __ __ __ __ CRITICAL

B. ECONOMY

1. The ability of the economy to maintain growth.

   LOW __ __ __ __ __ __ __ HIGH

2. The degree of government intervention in the economy.

   LOW __ __ __ __ __ __ __ HIGH

3. The ability of the government to set and meet economic goals

   LOW __ __ __ __ __ __ __ HIGH

4. The adaptability of the economy to various pressures.

   LOW __ __ __ __ __ __ __ HIGH

5. The degree of continuity in national economic policy.

   LOW __ __ __ __ __ __ __ HIGH

PART TWO: POLICY ISSUES

A. CRITICAL ISSUES: Please identify the three most important policy issues that might affect our operations in the Short Term (one to two years) and in the Long Term (two to ten years). For each issue, indicate the likelihood of a negative impact on our operations on a scale of seven by circling the appropriate.

	LIKELIHOOD OF NEGATIVE IMPACT ON FIRM (Low … High)
SHORT TERM (1-2 YEARS)	
1. ______________________	1 2 3 4 5 6 7
2. ______________________	1 2 3 4 5 6 7
3. ______________________	1 2 3 4 5 6 7
LONG TERM (2-10 YEARS)	
1. ______________________	1 2 3 4 5 6 7
2. ______________________	1 2 3 4 5 6 7
3. ______________________	1 2 3 4 5 6 7

B. KEY DECISION-MAKERS: Please identify, by name and position, the four government officials with the greatest influence over policy decisions affecting the automotive industry in your country, and their relative attitude toward foreign investors in the industry, on a scale from one (most negative) to seven (most positive):

	NAME	POSITION	ATTITUDE
1.	______________	______________	____
2.	______________	______________	____
3.	______________	______________	____
4.	______________	______________	____

OPPOSITION LEADERS: Please identify, by name and position, the four most important leaders outside government, in your country who influence decisions on these issues, and their relative attitudes toward foreign investors in the auto industry, on a scale of one (most negative) to seven (most positive):

NAME	POSITION	ATTITUDE
1. ____________________	____________________	____
2. ____________________	____________________	____
3. ____________________	____________________	____
4. ____________________	____________________	____

PART THREE: POLICY ENVIRONMENT

Please rank the situation in your country for each of the six issue areas listed below, on a scale of one (low) to seven (high):

ISSUE	RANK
Degree of Freedom of the Economy from Government Control	____
Degree of Freedom of Activity for Foreign Investors	____
Degree of Policy Continuity	____
Popular Support for Policies Favorable to Foreign Investors	____
Degree of Resistance to Political Change	____
Policy Influence of Financial Institutions	____
Central Bank	____
International Financial Institutions	____
Private Domestic Banks	____
Private Foreign Banks	____
Policy Influence of Private Sector:	
Domestic Firms	____
Foreign Investors	____

Selected Bibliography

Aharoni, Yair. *The Foreign Investment Decision Process* (Boston: Harvard University Press, 1966).

Alifano, Gerald. "A Reassessment of International Banking: A Regional Bank Point of View," in *The Journal of Commercial Bank Lending*, March 1984.

Beck, P. W. "Corporate Planning for an Uncertain Future," *Long Range Planning* 15, no. 4, 1982.

Bill, James and Robert Hardgrave, Jr. *Comparative Politics: The Quest for Theory* (Columbus: Charles E. Merrill Publishing Company, 1973).

Blake, David and Robert Walters, *The Politics of Global Economic Relations* (Englewood Cliffs: Prentice-Hall, Inc., 1976).

Blask, Jerome. *A Survey of Country Evaluation Systems in Use*, The Export Import Bank, December 22, 1977.

Brainard, Lawrence. "Bankers Trust Approach to International Risk Assessment," in *Assessing Country Risk*, Richard Ensor, ed. (London: Euromoney Publications, 1981).

Brewer, Thomas. *Political Risks in International Business: New Directions for Research, Management and Public Policy* (New York: Praeger Publishers, 1985).

Caldwell, J. Alexander. "Assessing Country Creditworthiness," *The Journal of Commercial Bank Lending*, July 1983.

Coplin, William and Michael O'Leary. "The World Political Forecasting Service," in *Political Risks in International Business: New Directions for Research, Management and Public Policy* (New York: Praeger Publishers, 1985).

De La Torre, José and David Neckar. "Forecasting Country Political Risk," in *The Handbook of Forecasting: A Manager's Guide*, Spyros Makridakis and Steven Wheelwright, eds. (New York: John Wiley and Sons, 1982).

Denison, Daniel. "A Pragmatic Model for Country Risk Analysis," *The Journal of Commercial Bank Lending*, March 1984.

Fagre, Nathan and Louis Wells. "Bargaining Power of Multinationals and Host Governments," *Journal of International Business Studies*, Fall 1982.

Fayerweather, John and Ashok Kapoor. *Strategy and Negotiation for the International Corporation: Guidelines and Cases* (Cambridge: Ballinger, 1976).

Friedman, Irving. *The World Debt Dilemma: Managing Country Risk* (Philadelphia: Council for International Banking Studies, 1983).

Gilpin, Robert. *U.S. Power and the Multinational Corporation* (New York: Basic Books, 1975).

Gladwin, Thomas and Ingo Walter. *Multinationals Under Fire: Lessons in the Management of Conflict* (New York: John Wiley and Sons, 1980).

Grayson, Leslie. *How and Who in Planning for Large Companies* (London: Macmillan, 1986).

Green, Robert. ''Political Structures as a Predictor of Radical Political Change,'' *Columbia Journal of World Business*, Spring 1974.

Grosse, Robert. ''Political Risk Evaluation Procedures Used in U.S.–Based Banks,'' in *Political Risks in International Business: New Directions for Research Management and Public Policy*, Thomas Brewer, ed. (New York: Praeger Publishers, 1985).

Grosse, Robert and John Stack. ''Noneconomic Risk Evaluations in Multinational Banks,'' *Management International Review*, January 1984.

Haendel, Dan. *Foreign Investments and the Management of Political Risk* (Boulder: Westview Press, 1979).

Hibbs, Douglas. *Mass Political Violence: A Cross-National Causal Analysis* (New York: John Wiley and Sons, 1973).

Huntington, Samuel. *Political Order in Changing Societies* (New Haven: Yale University Press, 1968).

Kennedy, Charles. ''The External Environment-Strategic Planning Interface: U.S. Multinational Corporate Practices in the 1980s,'' *Journal of International Business Studies*, Fall 1984.

Kennedy, Charles. ''Multinational Corporations and Political Risk in the Persian Gulf,'' *International Journal of Middle East Studies*, Fall 1984.

Knudsen, Harald. ''Explaining the National Propensity to Expropriate: An Ecological Approach,'' *Journal of International Business Studies*, Spring 1974.

Kobrin, Stephen. *Managing Political Risk Assessment: Strategic Response to Environmental Change* (Berkeley: University of California Press, 1982).

Kobrin, Stephen. ''Political Assessment by International Firms: Models or Methodologies,'' *Journal of Policy Modeling* 2, no. 3, 1981.

Kobrin, Stephen. ''Political Risk: A Review and Reconsideration,'' *Journal of International Business Studies*, Spring-Summer 1979.

Kobrin, Stephen, John Basek, Stephen Blank, and Joseph La Palombara, ''The Assessment and Evaluation of Noneconomic Environments by American Firms: A Preliminary Report,'' *Journal of International Business Studies*, Spring-Summer 1980.

Lecraw, Donald. ''Bargaining Power, Ownership, and Profitability of Transnational Corporations in Developing Countries,'' *Journal of International Business Studies*, Spring-Summer 1984.

Lomax, David. ''Sovereign Risk Now,'' *The Banker*, January 1983.

Mascarenhas, Briance and Ole Christian Sand. ''Country-Risk Assessment Systems in Banks: Patterns and Performance,'' *Journal of International Business Studies*, Spring 1985.

Mayer, Emilio. *International Lending: Country Risk Analysis* (Reston: Reston Financial Services, 1985).

Merrill, James. "Country Risk Analysis," *Columbia Journal of World Business*, Spring 1982.

Moore, Barrington. *Social Origins of Dictatorship and Democracy: Lord and Peasant in the Making of the Modern World* (Boston: Beacon Press, 1966).

Nigh, Douglas. "The Effect of Political Events on United States Direct Foreign Investment: A Pooled Time-Series Cross-Sectional Analysis," *Journal of International Business Studies*, Spring 1985.

Overholt, William. "The Scenario Technique," in *Political Risks in International Business: New Directions for Research, Management, and Public Policy*, Thomas Brewer, ed. (New York: Praeger Publishers, 1985).

Poynter, Thomas. "Government Intervention in Less Developed Countries: The Experience of Multinational Companies," *Journal of International Business Studies*, Spring-Summer 1982.

Poynter, Thomas. "Strategic Response to Government Intervention in Developing Countries," in *Political Risks in International Business: New Directions for Research, Management, and Public Policy*, Thomas Brewer, ed. (New York: Praeger Publishers, 1985).

Rayfield, Gordon. "General Motors' Approach to Country Risk," in *Assessing Country Risk*, Richard Ensor, ed. (London: Euromoney Publications, 1981).

Robock, Stefan. "Political Risk: Identification and Assessment," *Columbia Journal of World Business*, July-August 1971.

Root, Franklin. "Analyzing Political Risks in International Business," in *The Multinational Enterprise in Transition*, Ashok Kapoor and Phillip Grub, eds. (Princeton: The Darwin Press, 1972).

Root, Franklin. "U.S. Business Abroad and Political Risk," *MSU Business Topics*, Winter 1968.

Rummel, R. J. and David Heenan, "How Multinationals Analyze Political Risk," *Harvard Business Review*, January-February 1978.

Sachs, Paul. "Setting Country Limits: Approaches of Major U.S. Banks," in *International Political Risk Management: New Dimensions*, Fariborz Ghadar and Theodore Moran, eds. (Washington, D.C.: Ghadar and Associates, 1984).

Saini, Krishan and Philip Bates, "A Survey of the Quantitative Approaches to Country Risk Analysis," *Journal of Banking and Finance*, June 1984.

Schwendiman, John. "Managing Environment Risk: Cases and Lessons for Corporate Strategy," in *International Political Risk Management: New Dimensions*, Fariborz Ghadar and Theodore Moran, eds. (Washington, D.C.: Ghadar and Associates, 1984).

Sharp, Daniel. "Business Environment Assessment," in *Managing International Political Risk: Strategies and Techniques*, Fariborz Ghadar, Stephen Kobrin, and Theodore Moran, eds. (Washington, D.C.: Ghadar and Associates, 1983).

Spero, Joan. *The Politics of International Economic Relations* (New York: St. Martin's Press, 1981).

Tunney, Joseph. "Bank Perspectives in Measuring Risk," in *Assessing Country Risk*, Richard Ensor, ed. (London: Euromoney Publications, 1981).

Vernon, Raymond. *Sovereignty at Bay: The Multinational Spread of U.S. Enterprises* (New York: Basic Books, 1971).

Weber, Max. *Economy and Society* (New York: Bedminister Press, 1966).

Zink, Dolph. *The Political Risks for Multinational Enterprise in Developing Countries* (New York: Praeger Publishers, 1973).

Index

About the Author

CHARLES R. KENNEDY, JR., is an Associate Professor at the Colgate Darden Graduate School of Business Administration of the University of Virginia. He has contributed articles to the *Journal of International Business Studies*, *Middle East Executive Reports*, and the *International Journal of Middle East Studies*. He has also contributed chapters in *Political Risks in International Business*, and *International Political Risk Management: New Dimensions*.